Companion to

The Playboy of the Western World

Patrick Murray

THE EDUCATIONAL COMPANY

First published 1986
This reprint 1994

The paper used in this book comes from Managed Forests in Northern Europe For every tree felled, at least one new tree is planted

The Educational Company of Ireland
Ballymount Road
Walkinstown
Dublin 12

A trading unit of Smurfit Services Limited

© Patrick Murray, 1986

Approved Quality System

Cover Photograph: Playboy of the Western World, 1962 production directed by Brian Hurst. Photo courtesy of Pinewood Studios.

Design and Typesetting by Phototype-Set Ltd, Glasnevin, Dublin.
Proofreading: Clodagh Brook

Printed in the Republic of Ireland by
Citiprint Ltd., Dublin
0123456789

Contents

Act-by-act Analysis and Commentary • **5**

The Characters • **20**

The Playboy: A Comedy • **36**

The Serious Aspects of the Play • **44**

The Father-Son Relationship • **48**

Language and Imagery • **52**

Examining the Play • **58**

Critical Comment • **64**

Act-by-act Analysis and Commentary

ACT 1

PEGEEN AND HER WORLD (lines 1-219)

THE play opens with Pegeen Mike ordering her wedding garments from Castlebar, the nearest big town, along with three barrels of porter for the wedding reception. She is interrupted by Shawn Keogh, the man she is to marry. The contrast between the two is soon made obvious. She is lively, sharp-tongued and dominant; he is an awkward, timid, fearful, young fellow, lacking courage and determination. He has to wait a while outside the door wondering whether he is welcome to call. When he eventually comes in he talks mournfully and drearily about conditions outside ('I could hear the cows breathing, and sighing in the stillness of the air'). He talks and acts like a man old beyond his years. His words do little to reassure Pegeen, who complains that her father has left her alone in their isolated house to make arrangements with the friends who will accompany him to Kate Cassidy's wake, the big social event of the play.

Shawn is pleased to assume that when he marries Pegeen, she will not be lonesome, since he is not in the habit of attending 'wakes or weddings in the darkness of the night'. She playfully teases him for being so sure that she will marry him. At this point, however, she seems resigned to the prospect of Shawn as a husband, although the stage-direction, indicating that she answers him with scorn, suggests a less than warm feeling on her part for her admirer. She takes him for granted, and at his own low valuation of himself. If she marries him, it will only be because he is the best of a very bad lot of competitors. This is clear from her description of the other men of the district, who are cross-eyed, lame or mad. Shawn and herself, being cousins, will need a special dispensation from Rome if they are to marry.

Mention of this dispensation introduces the name of Father Reilly, who represents for Shawn the source of all authority on the important issues of life. Shawn's exaggerated deference to Father Reilly's views is to be the source of broad comedy in the play. Pegeen wonders, in her engagingly quaint and naïve way, how the Pope would pay any attention to a district like theirs, a place so deprived of human talent. Shawn characteristically is pleased enough with his surroundings and with the times in which he lives. Pegeen however scornfully rejects the present age as lacking in heroism and great endeavour and points to the achievements of notable men of the region in former days.

The passage in which she does this is typical of many in Synge. Her vision of heroism is absurd and grotesque and shot through with irony. One of her heroes knocked the eye from a policeman, another was jailed for maiming ewes and was famous for telling patriotic stories of 'holy Ireland' which drew floods of tears from old women. Everywhere in Synge we find incongruous juxtapositions like that of the barbarous acts of Sullivan and Quin with 'tales of holy Ireland'. Shawn thinks the countryside is well rid of such 'heroes', and comically invokes the authority of Father Reilly who would disapprove of people like Sullivan and Quin talking to local girls and presumably subverting their moral standards.

At this point however Pegeen is less worried about what Father Reilly may think than about her own security for the next twelve hours of darkness. She broadly hints to Shawn Keogh that he might stay and protect her. Shawn however pointedly ignores the hint; he would regard staying to protect Pegeen for the night as a major violation of moral and social codes, so he suggests fetching the Widow Quin. Pegeen dismisses the idea of the widow ('that murderer') as a companion, leaving Shawn to suggest that Pegeen's father, Michael James, might stay at home from the wake and protect her. This leads to Shawn's disclosure that he has just come across a fearful young man in a nearby ditch. Pegeen expresses concern for the man's plight and displeasure at Shawn's failure to see what ailed him.

The arrival of Flaherty and his cronies who are anxious to go to the wake leads to some humorous baiting of Shawn for not waiting to stay and protect Pegeen. Shawn's deference to Father Reilly's good opinion surfaces again and his fear of what the Pope and Cardinals might think of him if he stayed the night alone with Pegeen is an endearingly idiotic idea. Shawn is determined to resist all temptation and all force and persuasion to make him stay. He escapes from the shebeen without his coat threatening the curses of priests and bishops on the 'old Pagan' Flaherty. The latter expresses an ironical faith in Shawn's future fidelity as a husband and an ironical contempt for his virtue ('there's the coat of a Christian man'). Shawn quickly and fearfully returns pursued by the man he saw in the ditch. This is Christy Mahon, who enters at this point and is just as frightened as Shawn.

THE ARRIVAL OF CHRISTY (lines 220-445)

Christy's opening greeting ('God save all here!') is a grotesquely ironic one, coming as it does from a man who thinks he has recently killed his father. He makes a distinctly poor impression at first, with his wretched, dirty appearance and embarrassingly bashful manner. The suggestion that he may have been guilty of larceny calls forth his self-assertion for the first time, and also provokes his first lie, that he is the son of a prosperous farmer. Old Mahon, as we know from the list of characters, is, in fact, a squatter, a member of a deprived and despised class. This lie marks a turning-point for Christy, whose confidence grows with Flaherty's suggestion that his crime might be 'something big'.

Having dismissed the notion that Christy might be a petty criminal, Flaherty and the others are now prepared, with his co-operation, to accord him a higher status as a lawbreaker. He is imagined, for the moment, as a hero of the land war, who might have dealt the ultimate blow to those who deprived his father and himself of their lands. He is then considered as a possible counterfeiter, a polygamist, and a daring fighter for the freedom of the Boers.

His revelation that he has killed his father immediately changes the nature of his relationship with his interrogators. On his arrival he felt overwhelmed by them; now they are overawed by him. This revelation is also accompanied by a display of the kind of naïvety which is to characterise Christy to the end: he may have flattened his father with a blow of his loy, but he still sees himself as 'a law-fearing man', and is scandalised that he should be regarded as 'a slaughter-boy'. He tells another lie when he claims that he buried his father.

At this point, Pegeen is determined to have Christy under her roof, and comes up with the diverting suggestion that a man with the kind of talents he has displayed would make a splendid pot-boy. His status as a parricide seems to Pegeen, Philly and Jimmy to make him an ideal defender of the licenced premises and its occupants against the police, the army, the devil and the walking dead.

Pegeen has her own romantic reasons for employing Christy as a pot-boy. It suits Michael James and the rest to support her idea, because if Christy stays to protect her they can go with easy minds to the wake. As Jimmy puts it, with the absurd logic so characteristic of all the speakers in this scene, 'herself will be safe this night, with a man killed his father holding danger from the door'. Pegeen's next move, again a successful one, is to dispose of Shawn Keogh so that she can have Christy to herself.

THE TRANSFORMATION OF CHRISTY (lines 445-584)

The process of Christy's transformation can now begin in earnest. Pegeen's fascination with him has been clear from the beginning. Now when they are alone, she takes a proprietory interest in him, watches him delightedly, the daintiness of his feet and his impressive name, even hinting at a royal pedigree. Christy, who has already made himself the son of 'a strong farmer', now responds to Pegeen's fantasy by giving his family the status associated with the possession of 'wide and windy acres of rich Munster land'. Having now been dignified by this assumed heritage, Christy is further gratified to hear of his handsome features and 'noble brow'. All these qualities and assets which Christy is now beginning to believe he possesses, are enhanced by the flattering suggestion from Pegeen that his fiery temper indicates a poet's nature. Her vision of Christy living out his former days enjoying the company of women in the manner of 'a king of Norway or the Eastern world' is dispelled by his account of his dull, laborious existence, the highlights of which were the poaching of rabbits and the stabbing of a fish with a dungfork. By means of reductive images like these, Synge puts the heroic Christy in his proper context.

CHRISTY, MUCH SOUGHT AFTER (lines 585-725)

The entry of the Widow Quin is heralded by a farcical anti-climax of the kind Synge uses from time to time. Christy, convinced by Pegeen that he deserves a better life than he has hitherto enjoyed, is paying tribute to his own strength, manliness and bravery when he is interrupted by the Widow Quin's knock. This shatters his false courage, and he clings to Pegeen for protection. The Widow Quin quickly establishes herself as Pegeen's rival, and wants to bring Christy to lodge with her. She has come with the support of Father Reilly and Shawn Keogh, and is able to put up a spirited, though futile, struggle to get Christy for herself. Widow Quin is a shrewd, worldly woman who quickly realises that Christy is not the kind of dare-devil Pegeen thinks he is or wants him to be ('and you fitter to be saying your catechism than slaying your da'). The main feature of this part of the scene is the lively contest between the two women for the possession of Christy. This contest involves some extreme abuse on both sides, the most startling feature of which is the revelation that the Widow Quin performed a deed like Christy's but with more decisive results: her assault on her husband with a worn pick led to his death from corrosion of the blood. She is the only real murderer in the play, and, if Pegeen is to be trusted, a dabbler in the black arts and a woman of notoriously low moral standards. The impression she creates in this scene, however, belies the reputation Pegeen gives her. She is a strong, determined woman, just as spirited as Pegeen, and somewhat wayward, but still endearing, with her affecting talk of 'contriving' in her little garden, the attractiveness of her little house, and her pathetic consciousness of her loneliness. Her parting words about Pegeen's imminent marriage to Shawn Keogh cause alarm to Christy and embarrassment to Pegeen, who quickly and disingenuously dismisses the idea as 'lies and blather'.

By the end of the scene, Christy's fortunes have taken a considerable turn for the better. He came to the shebeen as a timid, dirty, wretched, hunted creature, with little hope and even less self-esteem. Now he can rejoice in the comfort of a clean, soft bed, and the consciousness that 'two fine women' are fighting hard for his affections.

ACT 2

CHRISTY AS THE ROMANTIC HERO (lines 1-215)

CHRISTY'S opening soliloquy illustrates his new sense of well-being and good fortune, and his enhanced self-esteem. A life of ease and idleness stretches before him; his days will be filled by pipe-smoking, drinking, conversing, and a little light work. Pegeen's tribute to his good looks is now something to be taken for granted ('Didn't I know rightly I was handsome'). The dialogue between the girls from the neighbourhood, who have come to take a look at Christy, gives the clue to the interest he has provoked. In this remote district, with its monotonous routine, new sensations are hungrily pursued. We learn that Sara Tansey once yoked an ass cart and drove ten miles to see the man who 'bit the yellow lady's nostril on the northern shore'. The attraction of setting eyes on 'a man killed his father' is even greater.

Pegeen and the Widow Quin have done much to minister to Christy's growth in self-confidence and self-importance. The village girls now intensify the process, bringing him presents and expressing their confidence in his ability to 'lick the world' when they find that Widow Quin has entered him in the local sports. Christy is flattered by the widow's request to hear the story of his encounter with his father. His first account of the event was short and concise. Now he elaborates and embellishes, adding dialogue, human interest in the form of Widow Casey, dramatic suspense, and colourful atmosphere.

The effect of Christy's story is to suggest an epic struggle between two powerful antagonists. It is worth noticing that this new version is not only much more elaborate than his first one; it is also different in one important detail, and this difference shows that Christy is less interested in telling the plain truth about what happened than in creating a romantic story with himself as hero. The first version merely had the loy falling on the ridge of Mahon's skull; this one also has him split to the knob of his gullet'. The response of his audience is the one he has come to expect: 'Well, you're a marvel! Oh, God bless you! You're the lad surely!'

ROMANCE FOR CHRISTY AND PEGEEN (lines 216-377)

Pegeen enters to find Christy, the Widow Quin and the village girls in riotous mood, arms linked and drinking a toast. Pegeen angrily orders the widow and the girls out. She is jealous, and responds sharply to Christy's talk of making himself presentable for the sake of 'the lovely girls' of the district. He wants to show again how he killed his father, but she impatiently dismisses his suggestion, telling him instead of the gruesome account of a hanging she has read in the papers. She warns him against giving the village girls any further details of his deed; they are in the habit of 'walking abroad with the peelers' at night, and may tell Christy's guilty secret and thereby get him hanged. This is sheer invention on Pegeen's part, inspired by her jealousy and possessiveness. Christy wonders if, in view of the danger posed by the talkative village girls, he should go on his travels again, and Pegeen pretends to think he should. This causes him to hint that she is an unfeeling creature ('It's more than Judges this place is a heartless crew').

At this point the tone of the scene changes, as Christy makes a strong appeal for Pegeen's sympathy. The key word in this part of the scene is 'lonesome', which occurs nine times in the space of just over thirty lines (302-38). Christy paints an affecting picture of his lonely life, passing small towns at night with only dogs for company, drawn to cities where his lonely heart pines as love flourishes all around him, looking back on a life of loneliness and deploring the fate that has made alienation from the rest of mankind his birthright. All of this sounds impressive, indeed almost heart-rending, and it has the desired effect on Pegeen. Much of it, however, particularly the account of nocturnal experiences in the vicinity of towns and cities, is difficult to reconcile with Christy's earlier affirmation that he never left his own parish until just over a week ago, and with his subsequent account of his eleven-day journey from the scene of his deed to Flatherty's shebeen, which featured him looking over 'a low ditch or a high ditch on my north or south, into stony scattered fields or scribes of bog' (Act 1, 484-6). At this stage, however, a sense of hard fact is what we least expect from Christy; the strength of his imagination is the source of his success.

His invocation of his loneliness, real or imagined, awakens a sympathetic response in Pegeen, who acknowledges that she too, has had a lonely life. This inspires an ardent tribute from Christy to her beauty and to the sweetness of her voice. Not to be outdone, Pegeen wonders how a 'coaxing fellow' like Christy 'with the great savagery' to destroy his father, could ever lack company. Christy suggests that it is time for him to leave forever if he is to avoid hanging. She is quick to restrain him, and, to his great joy, assures him of his safety if he stays. The prospect of working at her side, and watching her 'loafing around in the warm sun' by day and rinsing her ankles at night, makes his happiness complete. There is further reassurance in her flat declaration that she could have no regard for any man without the kind of bravery and spirit that he has shown. This declaration becomes ironically appropriate as Christy's rival, the timid and cowardly Shawn Keogh, runs in, followed by the Widow Quin. The widow and Shawn find an excuse to get Pegeen to leave.

SHAWN AND THE WIDOW IN COLLUSION (lines 378-503)

Shawn, fearful of losing Pegeen, is hoping to persuade Christy to leave the district for good. By way of a bribe he offers him half a ticket to America, some good clothes, and his blessing. Widow Quin supports Shawn's idea, in the hope that Christy may marry her if he cannot have Pegeen. She admits, however, to Christy's delight, that Pegeen is popularly believed to have decided on himself ('all is saying that she'll wed you now'). He accepts the loan of Shawn's clothes for the sports, wondering aloud what Pegeen will think of him in tweeds and a hat, thus convincing Shawn that bribery will not banish his rival.

Shawn, now desperate, entertains some futile thoughts of turning Christy over to the police, or running a pike into his side. Reminded that his lack of courage is his main disability in Pegeen's eyes, he relapses into comic fantasy, repenting the fact that, being an orphan, he cannot kill his father and so make himself 'a hero in the sight of all', as Christy has done. The Widow Quin raises his drooping spirits with the suggestion that she might marry Christy and leave Pegeen free for Shawn. In return she is offered a variety of attractive inducements.

Her best efforts to win Christy's affections are, however, unavailing; he makes it obvious that nobody interests him but Pegeen. He is by this time captivated by his astonishing success in winning acclaim and attention from all kinds of people. His sense of heroic grandeur, enhanced by his borrowed clothes, leads him to new heights of exaggeration. The blow that felled his father started as one to the ridge of the skull, and later split old Mahon 'to the knob of his gullet'. Now, his imagination in full flight, he tells the Widow Quin that he 'cleft his father, with one blow, to the breeches belt'.

OLD MAHON ON THE SCENE (lines 504-597)

Christy's passionate outburst of self-glorification is interrupted and made suddenly ludicrous by the arrival of old Mahon. This is the first comic climax of the play. It is also a turning-point in Christy's fortunes, since the foundation on which he has so elaborately erected his heroic reputation is now inevitably going to be undermined. The interlude between old Mahon and Widow Quin, with Christy hiding fearfully behind the door and having to endure the painful exposure of his heroic past, is rich in comedy, irony and suspense. Old Mahon, encouraged by the widow, provides an account of the Christy he has known; this makes an amusing contrast to the handsome young hero the villagers have created for their own admiration. Old Mahon's Christy is an idler, an incredibly incompetent farmer, a vain imbecile ('making mugs at his own self in the bit of a glass we had hung on the wall'), obsessively fearful of women, the standing joke of his native district. The physical descriptions are no more flattering: Christy is 'an ugly young streeler with a murderous gob'; he is small and low, dark and dirty, an ugly blackguard. All the irony of the scene is not at Christy's expense. The Widow Quin's delightfully ironic description of Christy turns the tables on old Mahon: 'A hideous, fearful villain, and the spit of you'. She sends the vengeful father off on a false trail, and stays to confront an embarrassed and troubled Christy, whose chief preoccupation is naturally with the effect old Mahon's reappearance and his story will have on Pegeen. For the Widow Quin, the main significance of old Mahon's return is that it gives her a ready and easy way to blackmail Christy.

THE WIDOW QUIN PROPOSES (lines 598-716)

The comic reversal of Christy's fortunes brought about by old Mahon's return has dramatically changed his relationship with the Widow Quin.

Up to now, although she may have doubted Christy's heroic credentials ('and you fitter to be saying your catechism than slaying your da'), she has treated him as a man apart, ministered to his self-esteem, and openly displayed her affection for him. For his part, he has been so preoccupied with Pegeen that he has had little or no time for the Widow Quin, and has made her only too well aware of his lack of interest in her as a possible marriage partner. She is now determined to use old Mahon's return and his revelations about Christy to her own advantage, her first aim being to persuade him to marry her. She is taken aback by Christy's vehement and sincere cursing of his father ('that the Lord God would send a high wave to wash him from the world').

The impulse behind this fierce hatred is soon obvious: Christy sees his father's return as the end of his present delightful relationship with Pegeen ('and now she'll be turning again, and speaking hard words to me'). The Widow Quin, tired of Christy's lyrical tributes to her rival, and finding it absurd that he should persist in seeing 'the love-light of the star of knowledge' shining from her brow, does her best to moderate his ardour by offering him a much less flattering and more down-to-earth version of Pegeen, emphasising her 'itching and scratching' and the 'stale stink of poteen on her'.

The widow makes her proposal of marriage, and offers Christy a future with her that has its own homely charms and its promise of romantic moments. Nothing that the Widow Quin can offer makes the slightest impression on Christy. His mind is still on Pegeen ('It's herself only that I'm seeking now'), and he begs the widow to help him to win her. The widow gives up the vain struggle for Christy's affections, but is determined to gain something for herself from her strengthened position. She wins from Christy the promise of a right of way, a ram, and a load of dung in return for giving a misleading account of old Mahon's identity ('We'll swear he's a maniac and not your da'). A relieved Christy rushes off to join Pegeen. The Widow Quin diverts herself with the thought that if Christy loses Pegeen, she herself will still be there 'to pity him', and, presumably, to win him finally for herself.

The Playboy of the Western World

ACT 3

THE THREAT OF DETECTION (lines 1-268)

LATER on the same day, Jimmy and Philly return from Kate Cassidy's wake, both slightly drunk. Michael James is too drunk to walk, and has to be brought home by Shawn Keogh in an ass cart. Jimmy and Philly discuss Christy's remarkable success at the fair and sports. Philly thinks that Christy's constant boasting about his brave deed may yet prove his undoing; Jimmy, on the other hand, suggests that since old Mahon's body must be rotten by now, there will be no evidence against Christy, who can't be hanged on the strength of his own story of the affair. Like the gravediggers in *Hamlet,* Jimmy and Philly talk about skulls and bones, most appropriately as it happens, since old Mahon has arrived in time to overhear them. When Philly mentions a remarkable skeleton he used to play with as a youngster, and claims that nothing like it can be found in modern times, the angry Mahon can no longer restrain himself, his own splintered skull, he suggests, is a unique specimen of its kind.

Neither Jimmy nor Philly knows that the intruder is Christy's father. When he reveals that the damage to his skull was caused by a blow from his own son, Christy's further exposure as a failed murderer seems imminent. The entry of the Widow Quin prevents this from happening, at least for the moment. Her role, at this point, becomes a crucial one. Only her presence of mind and quick thinking can save Christy from exposure. She does her best to convince Jimmy and Philly that old Mahon is a maniac who imagines that a tinker has cracked his skull, and that having heard of Christy's deed, he now thinks his son has done the damage. Jimmy, a man familiar with the vagaries of the human mind, is prepared to believe the widow's account, but Philly is suspicious, and it occurs to him to ask whether old Mahon has actually seen Christy, and to look for a description from him of his renegade son. Old Mahon's profile on his son as a contemptible fool does not match the Christy the villagers know.

Christy's luck is now running out. He is taking part in the mule race when old Mahon, seeing him from the window, is struck by his familiar appearance. Philly begins to assert himself against the Widow Quin, urging old Mahon to watch the race from a bench. Mahon takes a lively interest in Christy's achievement ('Good boy to him! Flames, but he's in!'), and suddenly recognises him ('It's Christy! by the stars of God!'). The reason for the identification takes some of the glory and dignity from Christy's athletic success ('I'd know his way of spitting and he astride the moon'). The Widow Quin now does her best to convince old Mahon that he is deluded, and he is inclined to agree ('I'm raving with a madness that would fright the world'). He is ready to go to the workhouse, and to leave the village stealthily and hurriedly to avoid the fate of an earlier maniac who, according to the Widow Quin, was hounded to death by Jimmy and Philly. Christy's safety from detection seems reasonably assured for the moment as the Widow Quin sees old Mahon on his way.

Philly, however, is to be the agent of Christy's exposure. He senses the truth about the relationship between Christy and old Mahon, and is determined to prevent the latter from leaving the district. Philly sees the possibilities for diversion in an encounter between father and son, and is ready to exploit them ('We'll have right sport, before night will fall').

CHRISTY'S 'CROWNING PRIZE' (lines 269-522)

Christy continues to enjoy his triumphs. He has been outstandingly successful at the sports, but he still thinks of his 'one single blow' to his father's skull as his most remarkable achievement to date. His 'crowning prize', however, will be Pegeen's promise to marry him. His speeches in the love-scene are stately in rhythm and exotic in imagery. Pegeen is sufficiently impressed to comment that a girl would 'walk her heart out before she'd meet a young man was your like for eloquence, or talk, at all'. The power of a lie and a fine command of words have already transformed Christy from a nonentity to a hero. Now his eloquence and imaginative power create a new Pegeen, a creature fit to take her place with Helen of Troy or with the heroines of romantic poetry. For all its poetic power, Christy's descriptive language tends to sound faintly comical. The exalted image of her as an 'angel's lamp' lighting the darkness becomes ludicrous when the same lamp is to assist him as he poaches salmon in the dark night. Whatever may be the effect of Christy's language on the reader, or the theatre audience, it impresses Pegeen. She accepts Christy unconditionally, and is prepared to ask her father for his consent when he has slept off the effects of his drinking.

Michael James arrives drunk from Kate Cassidy's wake, talking freely and embarrassingly about Christy's triumphs, his own enjoyment of the 'flows of drink' at the wake, and Christy's folly in not arranging a similar event for his father. Matters become critical for Christy and Pegeen when Michael James mentions the arrival, from Rome, of the dispensation which will enable Pegeen to marry Shawn Keogh. Pegeen declares that she will marry Christy and expresses her utter contempt for Shawn Keogh, whose great disability, in her eyes, is his lack of 'savagery or fine words', and his earthy, unimaginative nature. She points up a neat contrast between the two lovers: Shawn, preoccupied with the health of the livestock, would put a girl thinking about a bullock's liver; Christy would make her think of the lily or the rose. The ideal wife for Shawn, she rightly asserts, would be 'a radiant lady with droves of bullocks on the plains of Meath'.

Shawn is not prepared to challenge Christy for possession of Pegeen, preferring to live as a bachelor, 'simmering in passions to the end of time', than to face a dangerous enemy like Christy in physical combat. Michael James, conscious of Christy as a father-slayer, will not fight on Shawn's behalf. Pegeen's first suitor runs from the shebeen, abandoning his claim to her, and leaving the way open for the lovers to ask the blessing of Michael James on their marriage.

Christy now seems to have reached the pinnacle of his fortune; he is, in his own words, 'mounted on the spring-tide of the stars of luck'. Michael James pronounces his bizarre blessing on Pegeen and Christy. This blessing is an incongruous compound of crude images from horticulture and stock breeding ('peopling my bedside with puny weeds the like of what you'd breed, I'm thinking, out of Shawneen Keogh') and Christian prayers ('so may God and Mary and St Patrick bless you'). Like all the other serious utterances of the play, this one has its ludicrous aspects. Michael James, 'a decent man of Ireland', thinks that bravery is best exemplified in the kind of man who could 'split his father's middle with a single clout'.

CHRISTY AT BAY (lines 523-693)

Synge introduces his most exciting reversal of Christy's fortunes at this point. Just as the hero feels most secure in his prosperity and happiness, old Mahon appears for the third time. This development will, of course, have been vaguely anticipated by the audience since Philly's exit (Act 3, 262). Christy foolishly and unconvincingly tries to deny his relationship with old Mahon, but Pegeen speaks for the villagers when she exposes the hollowness of Christy's claim to heroic status: 'And to think of the coaxing glory we had given him, and he after doing nothing but hitting a soft blow and chasing northward in a sweat of fear'. In her contemptuous dismissal of Christy ('Quit off from this'), she repeats the formula Christy himself used in dismissing Shawn Keogh.

Christy is now at bay, without a friend to help him. The villagers want to see a fight between him and old Mahon. In a few defiant words he summarises his own recent history and the theme of the play. The villagers have made a mighty man of him by the power of a lie; they have given him a taste of the joys of company and social approval, but they have also shown themselves to be fools. In a final attempt to restore his lost glory and at the same time to regain Pegeen's love, he runs at old Mahon with a loy and appears to kill him. The Widow Quin, conscious that this act has even further alienated the villagers from him, and fearing that he may be hanged, tries unsuccessfully to get him away from the place, disguised as a woman. He does not want to leave without Pegeen; his feelings in her regard are expressed in the celebrated lines which provoked so much hostility during the earlier performances of the play: 'It's Pegeen I'm seeking only, and what'd I care if you brought me a drift of chosen females standing in their shifts itself; maybe, from this place to the Eastern World?'

It is ironic that the members of the community reject Christy when they come to think of him as a real murderer. His failed attempt at murder has brought him glory, so it is not surprising that he should imagine that a real murder, performed in the presence of witnesses, will restore his lost prestige. Pegeen makes it clear why this cannot be so. There is, she suggests, a world of difference between the splendidly-narrated story of a killing and the squalid performance of the same deed in the vicinity of one's home. In Christy's story, old Mahon was a villain of melodrama; now that the villagers have made his acquaintance, he is simply the victim of a bloody crime. Christy can expect no mercy from those he has antagonised; they prepare to deliver him to the police, and to what they assume will be death by hanging, mainly to save themselves from the punishment that may befall them as accomplices to murder. Michael James expresses their sense of communal self-interest: 'If we took pity on you the Lord God would, maybe, bring us ruin from the law to-day.'

THE OUTCASTS MOVE ON (lines 694-799)

The closing movement of the play involves a good deal of crude, boisterous horseplay, as comedy gives way to farce and burlesque. Christy is bound with a rope, is pulled to the floor, and twists his legs around the table. He gives a romantic, sentimental account of his imagined final moments on the gallows ('ladies in their silks and satins snivelling in their lacy kerchiefs, and they rhyming songs and ballads on the terror of my fate'). He bites Shawn's leg, and has his own leg burned by Pegeen who wants him to let go of the table. Old Mahon makes his fourth and final entrance, this time on all fours, and releases Christy. Father and son are reconciled after a fashion, but their relationship is changed. Christy, earlier transformed from a timid inhibited young man to a village hero, now becomes a third kind of man, a blustering bully like his father, whose master he will be from now on. He thanks the villagers for their part in shaping his character and destiny. Michael James prepares to resume drinking in peace, Shawn is glad he can wed Pegeen when his bite is healed and gets a box on the ear for reminding her, while Pegeen, the only loser, bewails her folly in letting go the only man who would have made her happy.

At the end of the play, the conventional inhabitants of the village are left in control, while the outcasts go on their travels. The Mahons, father and son, enjoy their special triumph, which is heavily underlined by Synge. The normal patrons of the shebeen are left to resume their drab, uneventful lives, and Pegeen must live with her grief and frustration. Old Mahon and Christy will enjoy themselves telling stories of 'the villainy of Mayo, and the fools is here', and live more freely and happily than those they leave behind.

The Characters

CHRISTY MAHON

FROM whining boy and dribbling idiot to self-confident romantic hero: such is Christy's progress. To make the transformation all the more striking, Synge affords us two detailed perspectives on the original Christy. His inadequacies are fully exposed on his arrival at Flaherty's shebeen, and his father offers a detailed account of Christy's earlier self, an account which matches the first impression he makes on the villagers. The early Christy is apologetic and self-pitying, speaks in a small voice, is afraid of being discovered by the police, and is far from eloquent or articulate. Old Mahon later fills out the portrait, heightening all the unflattering aspects of his son's character. He knows Christy as 'an ugly young streeler', an idle fool, fearful of females, the laughing-stock of four baronies, a small low fellow, drunk and dirty, a treacherous coward who struck a quick blow and ran.

The main theme of the play is the rapid development of this unpromising young man into the romantic, self-possessed figure who wins the admiration of the community and the love of two fine women. Synge does several things to make Christy's transformation credible. He makes him come to the right place, at the right time, and with the right qualifications for heroism in the eyes of the villagers. The two outstanding women of the district, Pegeen and the Widow Quin, are acutely conscious of the dearth of marriageable men; any newcomer is bound to attract favourable attention and excite curiosity. Christy has performed a daring deed in a fit of passion and is fleeing from the police; these circumstances are inevitably in his favour. His confession of parricide is received with open admiration. To the minds of the villagers, the slaying of a father represents the emancipation from authority for which they secretly long. When Christy eloquently describes his father's cruel tyranny, he earns sympathy as well as admiration. The villagers want a hero, and are prepared to give every encouragement to Christy's developing fantasy that he is one.

CHRISTY THE STORYTELLER

The vital element in Christy's evolution from timid nonentity to village hero is his discovery of his gifts as a storyteller. He finds himself among people who value storytelling, and particularly such accounts of marvellous deeds in distant places as he is able to give them. Under the pressure of their need to be delighted and entertained, Christy expands the significance of his deed and adds new details; as he does, he is enhancing his position in the minds of his listeners.

He wins a sympathetic response from the villagers to his first, and comparatively modest, account of the deed: 'I just riz the loy and let fall the edge of it on the ridge of his skull, and he went down at my feet like an empty sack'. Soon, he will offer an extended version of this, expanding his own role, and magnifying the force of his blow ('and he split to the knob of his gullet'). His final memory of the struggle involves the splitting of his father 'to the breeches belt'. He is encouraged to embellish his deed in this fashion by the delighted responses of his hearers to each new telling of his story ('That's a grand story. He tells it lovely'). He is surprised, as well as gratified, by the reaction of his audiences, and at their willingness to foster his illusions of greatness. He recalls with satisfaction that up to the day he killed his father, he was 'a quiet, simple poor fellow with no man giving me heed'. Now that he has told his story, he finds two fine women fighting fiercely for him, and his self-esteem growing by the hour.

THE 'POWER OF A LIE'

Those members of the community who regarded Christy as any kind of hero at the beginning are, of course, utterly mistaken. The part they play in creating his new self is, however, a vital one. Those who listen in awe of his story gradually convince him that he is a man of worth and substance, and as this conviction grows in him, he in turn is able to reinforce their belief in his heroism, and even to become the kind of man they mistakenly thought he was at the beginning.

Pegeen is the vital agent in the development of this process. From the beginning, she gives him an exaggerated estimate of his worth, and even of his appearance, suggesting, on the evidence of his 'little small feet' and his 'quality name' that he must have had great people in his family, and describing him as 'a fine handsome young fellow with a noble brow. Most of this is fantasy, but for Christy it represents a worthy ideal, and one he would, for Pegeen's sake, like to convert to reality. This is why he assures her that his family was indeed great, rich in the possession of great tracts of Munster land, and also why he indulges in comical acts of self-assurance: 'Didn't I know rightly I was handsome, though it was the divil's own mirror we had beyond, would twist a squint across an angel's brow'. His self-transformation occurs so that he may be able to live up to Pegeen's ideal of him.

In the end, Christy acknowledges that his heroic new self has been based on mere illusion; he can tell the villagers that they have made 'a mighty man' of him 'by the power of a lie'. Pegeen, too, in a most significant comment, pays tribute to her hero for having 'such poet's talking, and such bravery of heart'. It is not Christy's deed that matters to her, or to the others, but Christy's storytelling; brave talk is an adequate substitute for brave deeds in a community where imagination is starved, and where people will tend to welcome any kind of exciting diversion that will transform their dreary lives. Sara Tansey, we are told, journeyed ten miles in an ass cart to see the man who 'bit the yellow lady's nostril'.

Christy may have created his new self; or had it created for him 'by the power of a lie', but he becomes so attached to it that nothing that happens to expose the hollowness of his heroic claims can make him revert to his old self: the coward, the buffoon, the idiotic lout, 'the looney of Mahon's'. His achievements at the sports give him factual proof of his worth and ability, and reveal him to himself as well as to others as a hero in deed, and not merely in fantasy. After this, even his dreaded father cannot finally shake his confidence and his sense of self-importance, nor will he allow himself to be vanquished when his fragile claims to glory have been discredited in the eyes of the villagers. He will not tolerate any reduction in his hard-won status. He defies the villagers, and assumes the blustering, bullying tone previously associated with his father, whom he finally masters. Christy came to the shebeen insecure and dependent on the goodwill of the villagers; he leaves them feeling a hearty contempt for the folly of the very people who have helped to make him the man he is.

THE CREATION OF A 'NEW MAN'

Synge's presentation of Christy involves continuous use of contrast and reversal. Each phase of his career in the play contrasts with what has gone before or with what is to come. As Alan Price has pointed out, 'Christy's development from weakling to hero is a wave-like movement, an undulation with steep troughs, and the last and greatest wave, lifting him from the bottom of the deepest trough, throws up a new man'.

At the beginning, the timid, anxious visitor to the shebeen is at a low point in his fortunes, from which he is lifted by the welcome attention and admiration of Pegeen and the villagers. Then, as the Widow Quin knocks noisily at the door, his confidence and composure are shattered, and he is fearful, nervous and insecure once more. From this depth he is raised again by the spectacle of the two finest women in the district fighting hard for his exclusive attention. He reaches further peaks of self-esteem when he is exposed to the hero-worship of the village girls and the Widow Quin, but his confidence is quickly shattered by Pegeen's anger. This temporary fall from favour is followed by another steep rise in his fortunes as Pegeen asks him to stay. He continues to triumph. His improved appearance in Shawn's new clothes gives him added confidence, but the sudden arrival of old Mahon threatens to hurl him once more from the heights to the depths. The Widow Quin comes to his aid and his success at the sports gives his fortunes a new impetus.

Christy reaches the pinnacle of his success as he wins Pegeen's love, her promise of marriage and the blessing of her father. ('I'm mounted on the spring-tide of the stars of luck'). He is not allowed to enjoy his undreamed-of fortune. Old Mahon's reappearance dashes his hopes of marriage to Pegeen. He has nobody to help him in his final crisis; Pegeen and the villagers turn against him, and his luck seems to have run out. But his imagination and his newly-won sense of his own importance come to his aid. Spurred on by Pegeen's open hostility, he defies his tormentors, masters his father, and leaves the despised villagers conscious that he has triumphed over all adversity and become a new kind of man.

A HERO OF ROMANTIC COMEDY?

There are almost as many interpretations of Christy as there are critics. Some commentators have tended to take him and his achievements very seriously indeed, and to regard him as the heroic embodiment of passion and romance in conflict with the materialistic values of his society. To treat Christy as the hero of a romantic comedy, however, is to ignore the large farcical and mock-heroic elements in his role. His love-relationship with Pegeen, and his achievement of manly self-confidence, are consistently placed in a farcical context. His heroic pretensions are, it is true, expressed in stately rhythms and solemn cadences, but we are always aware of the ridiculous disparity between the noble, exalted style, on the one hand, and the character and achievements of the speaker, on the other. His famous lyrical set-pieces tend to overshoot the mark and tumble into bathos or anticlimax. His soaring celebration of Pegeen, with its poetic vision of 'the love-light of the star of knowledge shining from her brow' peters out in a reference to 'an old woman with a spavindy ass'. Pegeen will be 'an angel's lamp' to him with 'the light of the seven heavens' shining from her, but the 'light' turns out to be functional, rather than mystical, since it will further his success as a poacher when he is 'abroad in the darkness, spearing salmons'. Even his delighted contemplation of his future life as a 'gallant captain' to old Mahon's 'heathen slave' involves nothing nobler then seeing his father 'stewing my oatmeal and washing my spuds'. Christy's character has its most obvious parallel in the style of the play. This involves an incongruous juxtaposition of the ideal with the real, the high with the low, the noble with the base, the lyrical with the earthy.

PEGEEN

PEGEEN is a character who moves, emotionally, between two very different worlds, one represented by her first lover Shawn Keogh, and the other by Christy Mahon. Shawn is the embodiment of all that is safe and conventional, and is devoid of imaginative life and vigour. Christy comes to represent freedom, passion, poetry and irresponsibility. Pegeen, captivated by the dynamism and excitement of Christy's vision, eventually despises the unexciting Shawn, whom she has earlier been content, or at least resigned, to accept as a husband. But just as the delightful promise of happiness with Christy seems about to be realised, her hopes are dashed. She finds that Christy's account of his heroic deed has been false, and she comes to despise him too: 'It's lies you told, letting on you had him slitted, and you nothing at all'. Pegeen is, however, the victim of one of the supreme ironies of the play. She rejects Christy, calling him a 'crazy liar' because he has made her believe in the fiction that he has killed his father. But, as Alan Price points out, she fails to see that by means of this fiction acting upon Christy's imagination her image of a daring poet has become truth. Christy at the end really is the daring fellow she believed him to be, and he has become that without killing his father. Pegeen, in other words, is blind to the truth about Christy's transformation, and when she realises her error it is too late. Her wild outburst after he has gone conveys her sense of what she has lost through her folly. Hers is thus a tragic fate: an action undertaken in blindness has brought grave spiritual suffering upon her.

Pegeen plays a vital role in Christy's transformation. She presents him with a heroic image of himself from the start, and gives him a noble pedigree which is ludicrously at odds with his real one ('You should have had great people in your family, I'm thinking, with the little feet you have, and you with a kind of quality name, the like of what you'd find in the great powers and potentates of France and Spain'). She flatters his appearance, convincing him, in spite of his initial astonishment, that he is a handsome young fellow with a noble brow. His great desire is to make himself worthy of the image she has formed of him, and his one aim for the rest of the action is to impress her and show himself deserving of her love. Her power over his mind and heart is clearly demonstrated early in Act Two, when, after the Widow Quin and the village girls are sent away by Pegeen, he is left alone to face her jealous anger. When this has subsided, and when she makes it clear that she wants him near her from now on, his gratitude is overwhelming, as the stage direction '*(following her with fearful joy)*' indicates.

Just as Pegeen is an agent of major change in Christy's character and personality, he has a strong, and ultimately disturbing, influence on her spiritual and emotional development. Pegeen is a lively, proud, temperamental woman, whose early readiness to accept Shawn Keogh does not mean that she accepts the conventional code of values he stands for. Unlike Shawn, she looks with admiration to the adventurous, exciting, disreputable past represented by such 'heroes' as Daneen Sullivan and Marcus Quin. Christy appeals to the romantic, poetic side of her nature, and stimulates her imaginative fancies. His lyrical tributes to her beauty and his poetic declaration of his love inspire her to reveal her own secret desires: 'And myself, a girl, was tempted often to go sailing the seas till I'd marry a Jew-man, with ten kegs of gold'. At this point, she forgets her pride and her 'biting tongue', and openly and unashamedly reveals her feelings for Christy: 'I'll be burning candles from this out to the miracles of God that have brought you from the south to-day, and I, with my gowns bought ready, the way that I can wed you, and not wait at all'.

A SHATTERING OF PRIDE

Now that Pegeen has laid open her feelings, her pride is at stake, and the key to much of her behaviour towards Christy in the last movement of the play lies in her consciousness that her pride has been shattered by the revelation that Christy has deceived her about his achievement. Her wounded pride leads her to speak and act towards him with exaggerated vehemence. It is characteristic of her volatile temperament that when Christy proves not to have been the heroic kind of man her imagination had conceived him to be, she should dismiss him utterly ('It's lies you told, letting on you had him slitted, and you nothing at all'). Her offended pride is uppermost in her angry realisation that the world should see her 'raging for a Munster liar, and the fool of men', and in her thought that the discredited Christy is 'the one I'm after lacing in my heart-strings half-an-hour gone by'. What she does not realise, to her cost, is that while the bravery she admired in Christy was spurious, he has, at the moment of his rejection by her, really developed some of the manly qualities she has always respected. It is significant that it is her vehement attack on him that completes his transformation and rouses his fighting spirit to unprecedented intensity, as he spurns her ('That's your kind, is it?'), and faces the villagers defiantly and ferociously ('and shed the blood of some of you before I die').

PEGEEN'S LOSS

Pegeen is contrasted with the other village characters. She is more passionate, decisive and extreme than any of them, male or female, and her courage shows up the cowardice of the others, particularly of the men. It is she who blows the fire to scorch Christy's shins and who has to drop the rope over him when the men are either too drunk or too afraid to do so. She shows little respect for the main sources of authority, expressing contemptuous impatience at Shawn's reference to Father Reilly, and paying little heed to the authority of her own father, flouting his wishes with regard to her marriage.

In spite of the force of her personality and her masterful ways, Pegeen loses the love of the man who might have made her happy. The loss is partly the result of her hurt pride; it has also a good deal to do with the conservative, practical side of her nature. When her dream of Christy threatens to become a reality, she is unable to face its consequences. In the end, she is pathetically divided; having been unable to accept and recognise the new Christy until it is too late, she finds the prospect of his final and irrevocable loss utterly desolating.

OLD MAHON

CHRISTY'S father has a major function in the comic scheme of the play. His various appearances and re-appearances at vital moments provide a series of theatrically effective anti-climaxes which invariably provide hearty laughter at the expense of his unfortunate son. The most interesting things about old Mahon, however, arise from his developing relationship with Christy.

OLD MAHON, THE TYRANT

Early in the play, Christy makes it clear that his father has exerted a baneful, terrifying influence on his life; he presents old Mahon as a monstrous, unruly, destructive force, willing to destroy his son's happiness by forcing him to marry a repulsive woman and prepared to use brute force to establish his dominance. Christy provides a horrifying and extravagant account of his father as a drunken lunatic, rising at dawn and 'shying clods against the visage of the stars', never giving peace to anybody except when he is incarcerated in the asylum 'for battering peelers or assaulting men'. This account, the truth of which is substantially confirmed when old Mahon appears, is a useful part of Christy's early strategy. If he can claim to have killed such a formidable antagonist in single combat, his own physical prowess must clearly be thought of as remarkable, and he can present himself to the community as a conquering hero, a modern giant-killer. The presentation of old Mahon in this villainous light makes it easy for the villagers to excuse Christy's deed, since they must conclude that such a man as old Mahon deserves to die. It must also suggest to them that the son may have inherited some of his father's savage qualities, and make them all the more ready to accept Christy as a brave and reckless fighter.

Christy has rebelled against a tyrannical father, and proceeds to build a career on his heroic accounts of old Mahon's overthrow. In the shebeen, however, he soon exchanges one form of dominance for another. Having emancipated himself from his father's influence, he submits for a while to that of Pegeen, whose aim is to subdue him to her own purposes, and whose will is at least as strong as old Mahon's. Christy, however, comes to realise the futility of his love for Pegeen, and in a remarkable reversal of roles, achieves a dominance over his father with whom he is finally reconciled.

LIKE FATHER, LIKE SON

The father-son relationship is as central a feature of *The Playboy* as is the love theme. The early mutual expressions of fierce antagonism and contempt hide some fundamental points of similarity between old Mahon and Christy. Synge is careful to underline these. Mahon, like Christy, is an outcast, a lonely outsider and a vagrant ('I'm after walking hundreds and long scores of miles'). He also enjoys self-dramatisation and an appreciative audience ('winning clean beds and the fill of my belly four times a day, and I doing nothing but telling stories of the naked truth'). Christy will never let his listeners forget about his 'single blow' to Mahon's skull; his father is inordinately proud of the strength and endurance of the same skull ('tell me where and when there was another the like of it, splintered only from the blow of a loy'). Both father and son revel in exaggerated celebrations of their individual achievements and difficulties. If Christy can imagine with pride how he hit his father 'on the ridge of his skull, laid him stretched out and he split to the knob of his gullet', old Mahon can remember seeing 'ten scarlet divils letting on they'd cork my spirit in a gallon can' and 'seven doctors writing out my sayings in a printed book'.

The gradual identification of father with son is further underlined by the fact that, towards the close, as Christy contemplates the possibility that his rejection by the villagers may drive him back to a life of terrifying loneliness, he uses the kind of language and imagery we have come to associate with old Mahon: 'And I must go back into my torment is it, or run off like a vagabond straying through the Unions with the dusts of August making mudstains in the gullet of my throat'. Compare old Mahon's: 'And I after holding out with the patience of a martyred saint till there's nothing but destruction on, and I'm driven out in my old age with none to aid me'.

'GALLANT CAPTAIN' AND 'HEATHEN SLAVE'

There is more to the relationship between Christy and old Mahon than these striking resemblances. The movement of the play is towards a reconciliation between the two. There is a touching anticipation of this as old Mahon watches Christy's performance at the races. He does not at first recognise Christy, but has an uneasy feeling that the young champion is 'the likeness of my wandering son'. During the mule race, old Mahon's remarks suggest a quickening interest on his part in Christy's achievements ('He's passing the third ... Look at the mule he has, kicking the stars ... Good rider, he's through it again . . . Good boy to him! Flames, but he's in!'). This enthusiasm changes when he actually recognises Christy ('Let me out the lot of you! till I have my vengeance on his head to-day').

The climax of the relationship between father and son comes after Christy, having dealt old Mahon an apparently fatal blow, has been isolated from the villagers and rejected and betrayed by Pegeen, who burns his leg with a lighted sod. Old Mahon has come in unnoticed on hands and knees, and Christy, also on hands and knees, faces him. This time Christy is master ('Are you coming to be killed a third time, or what ails you now?'). He has overcome his fears, his inhibitions and his loneliness, and emancipated himself from all kinds of dominance. In his new relationship with old Mahon, Christy is to be the dominant figure. Mahon is at one with his son despising the fools and villains of Mayo, and calls Christy to come with him on his travels, when both will tell contemptuous stories of their experiences among the villagers. Christy, however, refuses to take orders from his father. He will go with him, but as 'gallant captain' to Mahon's 'heathen slave'. Mahon's 'Is it me?' marks a turning-point; he is now the minor partner, but his response to his new predicament is one of delighted surprise, as the stage direction *'(with a broad smile)'* indicates. His last moments in the play are happy ones. He knows that his son has at last achieved manhood, and is no longer the poor, timid, despised 'looney of Mahon's' but a spirited adventurer like himself.

THE WIDOW QUIN

THE Widow Quin is arguably the most interesting character in the play. Synge thought of her as a foil to Pegeen, but there are times when the sheer force of her exuberant personality tends to dominate the scenes in which she appears. She is significant in two ways. She functions impressively and convincingly as Pegeen's rival for Christy's affections, and, in common with old Mahon, adds a dimension of coarseness and satiric humour to the proceedings. She is a woman of experience, full of worldly wisdom, quickwitted and fond of intrigue. As well as being a foil to Pegeen, she is also a foil to Christy. It is sometimes forgotten that whereas he claims to have committed a murder, she has already performed a fatal deed; Pegeen reveals that she 'destroyed her man' by striking him with a rusty pick. Her gift for satiric humour is impressive. She strives to dispel romantic illusions whenever she discovers them in others. Fearful that Christy may become enamoured of Pegeen, she depicts her as an unsteady young girl who'd go 'helter-skeltering' after any man who would wink at her. Later, when Christy becomes intoxicated with Pegeen's charms and pays fulsome tribute to 'the love-light of the star of knowledge shining from her brow', the widow Quin takes malicious delight in providing a more earthy vision of her rival, 'a girl you'd see itching and scratching, and she with a stale stink of poteen on her from selling in the shop'.

If we are to believe Pegeen, the widow is a woman of notorious reputation and unseemly behaviour, dabbling, for example, in the black arts ('Doesn't the world know you reared a black ram at your own breast, so that the Lord Bishop of Connaught felt the elements of a Christian, and he eating it after in a kidney stew?'). She has been seen shaving 'the foxy skipper from France for a threepenny bit and a sop of grass tobacco', and lives in a leaky cottage whose thatch sprouts more pasture for her goat than do her fields.

A WOMAN OF IMAGINATION

Widow Quin, however, is more than a coarse-grained, satirical, ill-famed woman of the world. She is perceptive enough to recognise that the newly arrived Christy is not the kind of man who commits parricide ('and you fitter to be saying your catechism than slaying your da'). There is something appealing about her frank admission of her loneliness and desire for company ('... come on, young fellow, till you see my little houseen'), her talk of 'contriving' in her little garden, and her consciousness of advancing age. She is, too, a woman in whom both Christy and old Mahon can confide. She gives old Mahon an opportunity to express his feelings about his relationship with his son, and takes a maternal interest in Christy's troubles. Her relationship with Christy has its effects on her character. Under the influence of his imaginative fancies, she gives way to her own. Her acknowledgment of the joys and sorrows of her lonely life provides some of the most moving moments in the play. She has her good moments, 'odd times in great spirits, abroad in the sunshine, darning a stocking or stitching a shift'. At other times she looks wistfully at the passing fishing boats thinking of 'the gallant hairy fellows are drifting beyond, and myself long years alone'.

The Widow Quin becomes a key figure midway through the play when old Mahon returns, and Christy's destiny is in her hands. She does all she can to prevent the villagers from learning the truth about Christy, and she almost succeeds in getting old Mahon to leave the district without confronting his son. She shows presence of mind and quick wit in all her schemes, but in trying to spirit Christy away disguised as a girl, she fails to take account of the depth of his attachment to Pegeen. She contributes vitally to Christy's assumption of heroic status, and to his consequent self-fulfilment, since it is she who enters him for the sports.

A PRAGMATIST

Behind all her planning and contriving on behalf of Christy and Shawn Keogh the widow has her own interests at heart. She rejoices in the thought that if Christy loses Pegeen, she herself may win him ('it'll be great game to see there's none to pity him but a widow woman, the like of me'). In return for whatever help she may be able to give Shawneen Keogh in his efforts to win Pegeen, she makes him promise to give her a variety of valuable items and concessions; she elicits the same kind of promise from Christy. Unlike Pegeen and Christy, and like Shawn Keogh, she is able to accommodate romantic aspirations to everyday realities; if romance fails, she is prepared to bargain for material compensations. It is not the fault of her intelligence or ingenuity that her plans fail to materialise. She, like Pegeen, is defeated by the force of circumstances.

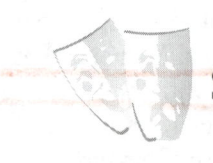

SHAWN KEOGH

SHAWN has a variety of functions. He is a foil to Christy, his rival for Pegeen, a provider of low comedy, and a representative of the values of his community.

The contrasts between Shawn and Christy are emphasised throughout. Shawn is a self-confessed coward ('I'd be afeard to be jealous of a man did slay his da'), and despised by the females of the district for his lack of spirit. The Widow Quin speaks on their behalf when she tells him that 'It's true that all girls are fond of courage and do hate the like of you'. Christy, on the other hand, is admired as one that has 'such poet's talking, and such bravery of heart'. Shawn is selfish as well as cowardly: he runs away from the man groaning in the ditch without a thought for his plight. He is unwilling to confront Christy in a fair trial of manly strength. He is also afraid to betray Christy to the police, not because he thinks this wrong, but because he may have to pay the price ('I'd inform against him, but he'd burst from Kilmainham, and he'd be sure and certain to destroy me').

SHAWN, THE VOICE OF CONVENTION

Shawn is a firm upholder of conventional values. Synge extracts much broad comedy from his repeated declarations of loyalty to Father Reilly and his firm support for the moral teachings of the Church. Shawn's Catholicism is caricatured throughout; his constantly-repeated fear of the consequences of Father Reilly's displeasure becomes a stock joke, and earns him the mockery and contempt of the other characters ('There goes the coat of a Christian man ... Go on, then, to Father Reilly, and let him put you in the holy brotherhoods'). Shawn's fearfulness of being rebuked by Father Reilly is carried to absurd lengths when he refuses to remain with Pegeen as her protector, in case he might upset the priest ('Let me out ... Oh, Father Reilly and the saints of God, where will I hide myself to-day?'). His attachment to a routine, formal religious code is comically and incongruously associated with base attitudes ('If I wasn't so Godfearing, I'd near have the courage to come behind him and run a pike into his side').

Christy stands for change and upheaval in village society; Shawn instinctively dreads any disturbance of the settled order of things. He is content and self-satisfied, totally devoid of romantic yearnings, and shows no sympathy for the prevailing glorification of the heroic past ('we're as good this place as another, maybe, and as good these times as we were for ever'). He loves Pegeen in his own pedestrian, unimaginative way, but he is not prepared to go to extremes to assert his claim to her against his dangerous rival. He would rather live a bachelor 'simmering in passions to the end of time', than battle with Christy for Pegeen. Even in matters of love, Shawn weighs, measures and calculates. His amorous nature is firmly rooted in the earth. As far as he is concerned, the drift of heifers and the golden ring he is offering have much the same status and significance as his 'weight of passion'. Pegeen can justifiably complain of him that he would put a girl thinking of a bullock's liver rather than of the lily or the rose.

MICHAEL JAMES

SHAWN Keogh describes Michael James as an 'old Pagan'; Michael James, with a touch of sarcasm, calls Shawn 'a Christian man'. Shawn's Christianity does not extend, in practice, very much beyond a fear of Father Reilly. The paganism of Michael James goes deeper, for all his drunken invocation of the 'blessing of God and the holy angels'; 'the will of God'; 'the name of God'; and 'God and Mary and St Patrick'. His life is centred on the enjoyment of 'flows of drink'; almost all his appearances feature him drunk, drinking or talking of drink. He regrets the lack of a decent burial for old Mahon mainly because, as a result, nobody can now drink 'a smart drop to the glory of his soul'. The highest compliment he can pay to the peelers is that they are 'decent droughty fellows'.

His paternal concern for Pegeen seems genuine, but he is prepared to leave her on her own during the hours of darkness in a remote shebeen while he goes to Kate Cassidy's wake to indulge his passion for liquid. He wants to prevent a murderous struggle between Shawn and Christy, because the shebeen is 'piled with poteen for our drink to-night', and a murder committed on the premises would spoil the festivities.

Michael James' sense of responsibility, then, is not highly developed. Like the Widow Quin, he does not worry about social respectability. His true nature is best revealed in his lengthy blessing of Christy and Pegeen, with its mixture of superficial Christianity and underlying paganism. His anti-romantic view of marriage and human relationships is the most obvious feature of this remarkable utterance (Act 3, 502-21). He was prepared to accept Shawn Keogh as a husband for Pegeen, even though he has obviously been troubled by the disturbing thought that her marriage to Shawn would involve her, as he puts it, in 'peopling my bedside with puny weeds'. There is no evidence that he is disturbed by the thought that her marriage to Shawn Keogh would be a loveless one. If Pegeen marries Christy, on the other hand, Michael James can look forward to seeing 'a score of grandsons growing up little gallant swearers by the grace of God'. His concern here, however, is less with Pegeen's happiness than with the breeding of suitable grandchildren.

A MORALLY AMBIGUOUS FIGURE

Synge gives Michael James a representative status as upholder of the values of the community. When the stability, and even the safety, of the community are threatened by Christy, Michael James knows that he has general support when he withholds mercy from the offender: 'If we took pity on you, the Lord God would, maybe, bring ruin from the law to-day, so you'd best come easy, for hanging is an easy and a speedy end'. Whatever unpleasant decisions Michael James takes, he passes responsibility for them to God, but the God he believes in is a morally ambiguous figure, like Michael James himself: 'It is the will of God that all should guard their little cabins from the treachery of law'.

The Playboy: A Comedy

ATTEMPTS to classify *The Playboy* are liable to run into difficulties. Synge himself was conscious of the problems people might have in trying to fit his play into one of the standard categories. In a letter to an admiring correspondent in 1907, he claims that he had written *The Playboy* as 'a piece of life', without thinking, or caring to think, 'whether it was a comedy, tragedy, or extravaganza, or whether it would be held to have, or not to have, a purpose'. The play has since been called a romantic comedy, a farcical comedy, an extravaganza, a burlesque, a satirical comedy, a tragicomedy, and a combination of some or all of these classifications. The earliest draft of *The Playboy* 'is headed *The Murderer (A Farce)*. Synge modified his original conception, and, as he pointed out in a letter to *The Irish Times* in 1907, *The Playboy* 'is not a play with 'a purpose' in the modern sense of the word, but although parts of it are, or are meant to be, extravagant comedy, still a great deal more that is behind it is perfectly serious when looked at in a certain light. That is often the case, I think, with comedy, and no one is quite sure to-day whether 'Shylock' and 'Alceste' should be played seriously or not. There are, it may be hinted, several sides to 'The Playboy'.'

ELEMENTS OF FARCE IN *THE PLAYBOY*

There are, however, large elements of farce in *The Playboy,* and these colour the play to such a extent, particularly in the final act, that it is tempting to call it a farcical comedy. Farce tends to provoke mirth of the most primitive and basic kind: simple, hearty and coarse. It is low comedy, involving exaggerated, often clownish physical activity, exaggerated characters and situations, improbable events, startling and unexpected appearances and disclosures, crude or boisterous jesting or broad humour, and a lack of subtlety as regards dialogue or plot. These elements may be found in every episode of *The Playboy*. The following are some examples.

(a) The stage-activity involving the 'temptation' of Shawn Keogh by Michael James, who tries to induce Pegeen's hapless suitor to stay the night in the shebeen, and ends up with Shawn's coat in his hands, as the terrified 'Christian man' disappears out of the door.

(b) The struggle between Pegeen and the Widow Quin for possession of Christy.

(c) The appointment of the 'hero' Christy as pot-boy ('That'd be a lad with the sense of Solomon to have for a pot-boy').

(d) Christy's futile and embarrassed attempt to hide the looking-glass from the village girls.

(e) The Widow Quin and Christy dancing and drinking with their arms linked 'like the outlandish lovers in the sailor's song'.

(f) Old Mahon's first appearance at the height of one of Christy's flights of self-glorification. The terrified son has to hide behind the door and listen to a most unheroic account of his past life.

(g) Jimmy and Philly, talking about remarkable skeletons, interrupted by an angry old Mahon who regards his own splintered skull as a match for anything yielded up by the past.

(h) Mahon's heightened account to the Widow Quin of his bouts of madness ('there I was one time, screeching in a straightened waistcoat, with seven doctors writing out my sayings in a printed book').

(i) The return of Michael James from the wake, with his drunken, incongruous talk and behaviour.

(j) The absurd encounter between Christy and Shawn as they stage their unequal fight for Pegeen. This involves a good deal of pushing, and violence which is threatened but not inflicted. The stage directions indicate the farcical quality of the episode. Christy speaks 'with ferocity'; Michael James springs up 'with a shriek' and pushes Shawn towards Christy; Shawn shakes himself free and gets behind Michael James, who again pushes him forward to fight Christy. The latter takes up the loy and Shawn 'flies out of the door'.

(k) Flaherty's farcical blessing of Christy and Pegeen is immediately followed by the violent, melodramatic entry of old Mahon, who knocks Christy down and beats him. This in turn is followed by a long passage of violent gestures and threatening postures, culminating in Christy's second blow to Mahon's head with the loy.

(l) With the efforts of the Widow Quin and Sara to save Christy from the law, we reach new depths of farce. They try to dress their hero in Sara's petticoat and shawl, but he defies their efforts, threatening them with a stool.

(m) The stage-activity involving the tying of Christy with a rope, and the bouts of horseplay which follow, are crude and unsophisticated examples of low comedy, in which the whole emphasis is on violent action and sensation.

(n) There is a further deterioration in the comic tone of the play as Christy, having twisted his legs around the table, squirms on the floor and bites Shawn's leg, only to have his own leg burned by Pegeen's lighted sod.

(o) The final encounter between Christy and old Mahon involves further horseplay. Old Mahon comes in on all fours, and Christy scrambles on his knees to free him, wondering if he is coming 'to be killed a third time'. Christy's heroic pretensions to mastery over his father are expressed in farcical terms: old Mahon will be condemned to 'stewing my oatmeal and washing my spuds'.

FARCICAL STYLE AND LANGUAGE

The proportion of farcical material in *The Playboy* is thus very large indeed, and such material is the source of much of the comic effect. Farcical action is matched by Synge's farcical style, which involves the continuous juxtaposition of conflicting and oddly-assorted ideas and phrases for comic and satiric purposes. Pegeen's notion of heroism is an early example: her two heroes of the past are violent, dangerous men whose activities and personalities she nevertheless invests with a vaguely religious significance. Daneen Sullivan maimed a peeler and Marcus Quin maimed ewes: in Pegeen's eyes, however, they are in good standing with God and 'holy Ireland'. Christy Mahon, who supposes himself a murderer, greets the company in the shebeen with 'God save all here!', and he answers the astonished Pegeen, who expresses incredulity at the notion that he could have killed his father, in characteristically incongruous fashion: 'With the help of God I did surely'. In a world where logic and reason play so small a part, we are not surprised to hear Jimmy declare, 'by the grace of God', that Pegeen is bound to be safe 'with a man killed his father holding danger from the door'. And Christy, who glories in his role as slayer of his father with a loy, is deeply offended when Pegeen wonders if he shot him ('I've no licence, and I'm a law fearing man'), and when Michael suggests that he may have stabbed him ('Do you take me for a slaughter-boy?'). By now, we have come to expect violent deeds receiving religious sanction. 'Oh, God bless you!' is the response of the girls to Christy's account of his stretching out of old Mahon, 'and he split to the knob of his gullet'.

Sometimes, too, Synge provides a religious setting for something contrary not only to religion but to human decency, as in Flaherty's account of the mourners at Kate Cassidy's graveside, 'stretched out retching speechless on the holy stones', and his notion that old Mahon's burial must involve 'a Christian drinking a smart drop to the glory of his soul'. The odd mixture of Christian and pagan elements reaches its climax in Flaherty's blessing of Pegeen and Christy, which features the use of Christian formulae ('the will of God'; 'the name of God'; 'God and Mary and St Patrick bless you'), to disguise some thoroughly un-Christian notions of love and marriage. Flaherty also invokes blessings on the man who has been brave enough 'to split his father's middle with a single clout', and seems to find divine approval for every kind of lawlessness ('It is the will of God that all should guard their little cabins from the treachery of law').

ANTI-CLIMAX AS A COMIC DEVICE

Related to this absurd counterbalancing of discordant ideas is another of Synge's comic devices, used at many points in the play. This is anti-climax, both of action and language. Anti-climax involves a ludicrous drop in impressiveness following a progressive rise, and is repeatedly used by Synge in *The Playboy* to speed up the farcical side of the action. Christy is its main victim. Just when he is most eloquently celebrating his own heroism and strength, something invariably happens to diminish or shatter his sense of self-importance, and always with comic effect. In the first Act, he is reaching new heights of self-importance, telling Pegeen of his bravery, when the Widow Quin's knocking reduces him to terror. He has recovered sufficiently by the middle of the second Act to provide his enthralled listeners with an exaggerated account of his manly prowess as a murderer, when his supposed victim suddenly appears and forces him to hide behind the door. Synge makes further effective use of anti-climax in Act Three. When Christy seems to be 'mounted on the spring-tide of the stars of luck', and has won the consent of Michael James to marry Pegeen, old Mahon suddenly arrives to shatter his good fortune.

Synge seems anxious at all times not to let the 'serious' or pretentious side of Christy's relationship with Pegeen get too far, nor will he allow Christy to achieve undue dignity as a hero. Christy's mock-heroic status is preserved partly through the consistent use of anti-climax as a feature of his speeches, and partly through placing even his most solemn utterances and serious achievements in a ludicrous context. Christy achieves an impressive lyrical style in his speeches to and about Pegeen, but his poetic outbursts often peter out in banality. He begins one inspiring speech, for example, with a visionary glimpse of 'the love-light of the star of knowledge' shining from Pegeen's brow, but ends it with the image of 'an old woman with a spavindy ass'. The lyricism of the same speech is further undercut by the Widow Quin's disenchanted view of Pegeen as an itching, scratching creature exuding 'a stale stink of poteen. A later reference to 'the light of the seven heavens' shining from Pegeen's heart like a lamp, takes on an absurd aspect when Christy seems to think of the same light as an aid to his nocturnal salmon-poaching. And Christy's crowning achievement, his victory in the mule-race, loses much of its dignity when old Mahon provides the commentary: 'It's Christy! by the stars of God! I'd know his way of spitting and he astride the moon!'

THE PLAYBOY AS A SATIRIC COMEDY

There are important elements of satiric comedy in *The Playboy*. The vices, follies and absurdities of the rural community are ridiculed, and the stupidity and narrow views of its members are exposed to scorn. Shawn Keogh is the chief satiric victim, and through him the Catholic Church, personified by the absent but frequently-invoked Father Reilly, is exposed to mildly ironic scrutiny. Shawn's outlook is that of a faithful, loyal member of the Church, submissive in all things to the direction of Father Reilly. For his repeated emphasis on his fear of Father Reilly and of 'the Holy Father and the Cardinals of Rome', Shawn is made a figure of fun, and, by extension, the objects of his admiration and awe are made to seem faintly ridiculous. Both Pegeen and the Widow Quin are prepared to mock the authority of the priests, and in this they have the emotional weight of the play behind them. 'Go on then to Father Reilly', Pegeen, tells Shawn, 'and let him put you in the holy brotherhoods', while the Widow Quin, with a touch of sarcasm, refers to Shawn as 'the priesteen'.

The religious sense of the community is, as some early opponents of the play realised, revealed by Synge as being primitive and inadequate. Michael James has a pagan conception of life, love and marriage. Shawn Keogh's Christianity seems to involve no more than fear of the priest, while Sara Tansey has a ludicrous notion of the meaning of basic Church doctrine: 'You'd be ashamed this place, going up winter and summer with nothing worth while to confess at all'. Synge's sidelong satiric glance at the Catholic Church was one of the aspects of the *The Playboy* which attracted unfavourable critical comment in the early days. Indeed, there are times when religious satire in *The Playboy* seems to involve something more fundamental than the practices of the Church and the ignorance and stupidity of some of its members. Christy, despite the implications of his Christian name, is allowed to express irreverently pagan sentiments about the Deity; at one point he suggests that God himself, 'sitting lonesome in his golden chair', might have cause to envy the happiness of mortal lovers. Soon after this, he shares with Pegeen his extraordinary vision of the 'holy prophets' of Christianity 'straining the bars of Paradise' to get a glimpse of the pagan Helen of Troy.

There are other targets for satire in the play. Lack of respect for an alien system of law and for the British administration are clearly articulated from time to time. We find Pegeen referring bitterly to the 'thousand militia – bad cess to them! – walking idle through the land', and to the 'loosèd khaki cut-throats' of the British army. She admires major infractions of the law, and regards the knocking of the eye from a peeler and the maiming of ewes as worthy, even heroic, achievements. Jimmy Farrell is prepared to expose his dog to a cruel death to avoid paying a licence-fee for it, while the police, if we are to believe Michael James, take their duties lightly: 'the peelers in this place is decent droughty poor fellows, wouldn't touch a cur dog and not give warning in the dead of night'. All of these satirical elements have a decidedly comic dimension.

A SENSE OF THE MACABRE

Much of the humour of *The Playboy* is macabre and grotesque. Synge, following folk tradition, freely exploits the comic possibilities of ugliness, cruelty and suffering. A passage from his book on the Aran Islands illustrates the folk background to the cruel humour we find in *The Playboy*:

> Although these people are kindly towards each other and to their children, they have no feeling for the suffering of animals, and little sympathy for pain when the person who feels it is not in danger. I have sometimes seen a girl writhing and howling with toothache while her mother sat at the other side of the fireplace pointing at her and laughing at her as if amused by the sight.

The treatment of painful, unhappy and gruesome situations as matter for laughter is a recurring motif in *The Playboy*. The comic implications of parricide are pursued with considerable thoroughness, and various versions of Christy's murderous deed are recorded in graphic detail, always with comic overtones. Murder, as Christy visualises it (with the victim 'split to the knob of his gullet'), is a ludicrous rather than a criminal deed. The comic treatment of Christy's act of parricide is matched by similar treatment of the Widow Quin's destruction of her husband. Pegeen's account of that cruel deed invariably provokes laughter: 'She hit himself with a worn pick and the rusted poison did corrode his blood the way he never overed it'. Those who can inflict suffering on man or beast are, in the macabre universe of *The Playboy,* to be admired, even revered, like Daneen Sullivan and Marcus Quin, and their exploits, presented in a comic context, are described in such a way that one's only possible response is to laugh ('Where now will you meet the like of Daneen Sullivan knocked the eye from a peeler?'). The same black, grotesque comedy is wrung from such infernal cruelties as that inflicted by Jimmy Farrell on his dog ('had it screeching and wriggling three hours at the butt of a string'), and from the fate of the little laying pullet 'crushed at the fall of night by the curate's car'. Sometimes, Synge draws his comic effects from exaggerated outbursts of verbal violence, as when Christy imagines old Mahon threatening to flatten him out 'like a crawling beast has passed under a dray'. Ugliness and unhappiness are also exploited by Synge for comic purposes.

This is a characteristic feature of his presentation of old Mahon, who acknowledges that he is 'raving with a madness that would fright the world' but whose predicament is made to generate hearty laughter rather than pity. Mahon's madness, induced by his drinking himself 'silly and parlatic from dusk to dawn', is celebrated by its victim in grotesquely comic language. He is childishly proud of his status as 'a terrible fearful case', lovingly recalling his demented hallucinations involving 'rats as big as badgers sucking the life blood from the butt of my lug', and the interesting time he spent 'screeching in a straightened waistcoat' having his sayings copied out by seven doctors. Repulsive human images characterise another of Synge's comic fantasies: Christy's inspired description of the Widow Casey, 'two hundredweights and five pounds in the weighing scales, with a limping leg on her and a blinded eye'.

The Serious Aspects of the Play

LIKE almost every comedy, *The Playboy* has its serious side. Early Irish audiences took the play very seriously indeed. It is clear from public reaction to early productions that Synge's contemporaries thought he was offering a serious critique of Irish life rather than an extravaganza or a farce. Many of those who objected to *The Playboy* did so because they felt that Synge did not present a true impression of Irish life, and that his play was an insult to the Irish peasantry and to Irish womanhood. Newspaper reviews, letters to newspaper editors, and the riotous behaviour of theatre audiences strongly suggest a widespread belief that Synge meant Christy, Pegeen and the Widow Quin to be taken seriously as Irish peasant types. Most of those who commented publicly were outraged by what they took to be Synge's ignorance, or his offensive malice. How, it was asked, could an Irish dramatist represent Irish people actively sympathising with a parricide, and Irish girls throwing themselves into his arms? Those patriots who were offended by the play angrily pointed out that in no part of Ireland would women be found so lacking in modesty as to make advances to a total stranger, let alone to a criminal. In no part of the South or West, they contended, would a parricide like Christy be welcomed; on the contrary, he would be shunned, and his relations boycotted for generations. In general, Synge's hostile critics felt that he had sacrificed truth and decency, and perpetrated a gross calumny on Irish rural life.

The standard answer to such criticisms is that those who made them were taking Synge's play too seriously, not realising that *The Playboy* was an extravagant comedy, almost a fantasy, and not by any stretch of the imagination a realistic comment on rural Ireland in the first decade of the twentieth century. Synge himself, in a letter to *The Irish Times,* pointed out that he had not written a play with a purpose or a thesis in mind. More significantly, he claimed that although parts of *The Playboy* 'are, or are meant to be, extravagant comedy, still a great deal that is in it, and a great deal more that is behind it, is perfectly serious, when looked at in a certain light'.

This is a vital observation. The play features a good deal of at least potentially serious matter. When Synge talked about looking at *The Playboy* 'in a certain light' and finding it serious, he was taking account of the fact that the same work can give rise to radically differing interpretations, depending on the background, point of view, sensibilities, and even the sense of humour of the interpreters.

THE TRAGEDY OF PEGEEN'S PREDICAMENT

Some examples will illustrate the truth of this. In many accounts of the play, the Christy-Pegeen relationship is treated with utter seriousness, even solemnity. Critics are liable to picture the two as star-crossed, almost tragic, lovers, whose happiness is inevitably thwarted by the hostile, unromantic world represented by Michael James and Shawn Keogh. From Pegeen's point of view, there is certainly a serious dimension to the affair. Christy may enter her life as a paradoxically boastful and timid parricide, but he soon appears to her as the first man to whom she can give her heart without reserve, as her lyrical tributes to his manly qualities testify ('and any girl would walk her heart out before she'd meet a young man was your like for eloquence, or talk, at all'). The sophisticated reader or spectator may find such utterances faintly comic or even ludicrous, but it expresses Pegeen's true feelings. The intensity of these feelings becomes very obvious after Christy's claims as a parricide have been exposed as false.

Pegeen's rage at being deceived is fierce and bitter. Love momentarily turns to hatred and contempt as she gives vent to hurt pride. Her natural instinct is to bring about Christy's destruction, her chief motives for this being his betrayal of her and her wounded pride. She expresses her angry frustration with an intensity that one does not associate with conventional comedy. She is anxious to see Christy suffer at

Mahon's hands: 'It's there your treachery is spurring me, till I'm hard set to think you're the one I'm after lacing in my heart-strings half-an-hour gone by'. The seriousness of Pegeen's predicament when she can no longer respect and admire Christy as a hero must be appreciated if we are to understand the tragic, or at least the sub-tragic dimensions of the play. From the beginning it is clear that Pegeen admires men of action capable of heroic deeds and despises those who, like Shawn Keogh, conform fearfully to conventional standards. For a short, joyful couple of days she thinks she has found a man worthy of her highest hopes; to find these hopes dashed is a shattering blow, particularly as this will inevitably consign her to a monotonous and cheerless life among people she will now regard with contempt and disgust in the light of her experience, however illusory, of something nobler and higher. Whatever tragic dimension is to be found in the play is associated with Pegeen's predicament.

A CRITIQUE OF LIFE ON THE WESTERN SEABOARD

It is quite possible to discover a serious side to Synge's depiction of life on the Western seaboard. Anybody with taste, refinement or moral sense will tend to regard the presentation of Michael James and his associates with some measure of abhorrence, while still relishing the comedy with which Synge invests them and their way of life. There is an underlying element of satire in Synge's rendering of the world that finds its centre in the shebeen, and its main source of gratification in what Pegeen's odious, disreputable father calls 'flows of drink'. Depending on one's point of view, one can find the following account of Kate Cassidy's wake and its aftermath either grotesquely comic or seriously disturbing; some generously inclusive sensibilities may be able to accommodate both kinds of response at the same time: 'for you'd never see the match of it for flows of drink, the way when we sunk her bones at noonday in her narrow grave, there were five men, aye, and six men, stretched out retching speechless on the holy stones'. The brilliant technical virtuosity of this passage, with its splendid collocation of matching sound-patterns, cannot fully conceal its revolting implications, the grisly spectacle of human beings debasing themselves by vomiting uncontrollably on gravestones. Again, Flaherty's comic status cannot fully mitigate the disgust inspired by his foul-mouthed apologies for a totally amoral code of behaviour, his equation of love and marriage with plant-breeding ('peopling my bedside with puny weeds the like of what you'd breed, I'm thinking, out of Shawneen Keogh') and his animal images of human beings (a bachelor as a 'braying jackass').

LIVES WHICH INSPIRE PITY

There is a serious aspect to the presentation of old Mahon, whose alcoholism has driven him to the verge of madness, and sometimes beyond. Again depending on one's point of view, his description of his lunacy and incarceration in institutions can provide material for laughter. Synge gives a comical twist to Mahon's heroic account of his adventures with the medical profession ('and I a terrible and fearful case, the way that there I was one time, screeching in a straightened waistcoat, with seven doctors writing out my sayings in a printed book'). Those who do not regard insanity as an appropriate subject for comedy may well take a different view, and find Mahon a disturbing, pathetic character, meriting pity rather than laughter.

There is also a serious side to the Widow Quin, whose frustrated yearnings for a more romantic way of life make her more than a merely comic figure. Like old Mahon, she can inspire pity as she shares with Christy her longings, her varying moods, and her deep sense of loneliness:

> I'm above many's the day, odd times in great spirits, abroad in the sunshine, darning a stocking or stitching a shift, and odd times again looking out at the schooners, hookers and trawlers is sailing the sea, and I thinking on the gallant hairy fellows are drifting beyond, and myself long years living alone.

The notion of a fine, spirited woman like the Widow Quin passing her days in the solitary contemplation of hopes she can never realise is a pathetic one. Her good-humoured, futile stratagems to win Christy's affection are also touched with pathos as is the close of the play, when Pegeen is left to face the intolerable prospect of sharing her life with a man for whom she can feel only the profoundest distaste.

The Father-Son Relationship

THE father-son relationship is a central theme of *The Playboy*. Everything that happens in the play is influenced by Christy's relationship with old Mahon. The fateful blow of the loy to Mahon's head, which is a blow for freedom from an oppressive dominance of father over son, forces Christy to flee from home, and leads on to a chain of circumstances which will change his life: his arrival in Mayo, his discovery of Pegeen, his emergence as a heroic personality and his liberation from his father's control. Even as Christy enjoys the fruits of his heroic reputation in Mayo, he is haunted by the fear that his father may come and depose him from his newly-acquired eminence.

OLD MAHON'S DOMINANCE

In its earlier phases, the father-son relationship is an unequal one. Old Mahon depicts himself and is depicted by Christy, as a tyrannical father who can exercise effortless control over a spineless, timid son. The father takes his dominance for granted and, until Christy strikes his blow with the loy, encounters no opposition from his son. Christy's own account of the incident which leads him to strike his father makes it clear that up to this the latter has been the master and he the slave. Mahon has taken his mastery over Christy so much as a matter of course that he feels able to order him about as he pleases. As an exercise in the enforcement of his authority, he approaches him in the potato field and orders him to get married speedily to the repulsive Widow Casey. He is so enraged by Christy's unexpected resistance to this proposal that he makes angry and violent threats ('... go on now or I'll flatten you out like a crawling beast has passed under a dray ... I'll have the divil making garters of your limbs to-night').

Old Mahon's highly-coloured account of Christy suggests his utter contempt for his son. He has obviously always regarded him as a contemptible waster, 'a lier on walls, a talker of folly, a man you'd see stretched the half of the day in the brown ferns with his belly in the sun'. Christy's blow to his father's head is to change this relationship, but not immediately. By the time old Mahon arrives at the shebeen, his son has not yet shaken off his servitude. Christy is in dread of the consequences of an encounter with his father ('Where'll I hide my poor body from that ghost of hell?'). His main concern, however, is that Mahon will expose the falsity of his heroic stories about the slaying in the potato field and that, as a result, Pegeen will despise and reject him.

CHRISTY'S LIBERATION

Christy's experiences in the shebeen since his arrival have, however, made it unlikely that old Mahon will ever again be able to dismiss him with contemptuous disdain. Through the power of eloquent language, or, as he himself puts it, 'the power of a lie', Christy creates for himself a new personality and independence. He is helped in this by the exaggerated admiration of the young women of Mayo: Pegeen, the Widow Quin, Sara, Susan and the rest. Once Christy has cast himself in the heroic mould, he is most unwilling to revert to his previous status as a timid, tearful coward, subservient to his father's angry whims. He enjoys being a hero, and is eventually prepared to act like one rather than forfeit his claims on the admiration of the community. His final confrontation with old Mahon shows a growing awareness on Christy's part that he must play a man's role and outface his father if he is not to spend the rest of his life in fear of old Mahon and feeling contempt for himself. First he wants the Widow Quin to protect him by coming between him and his father. But his angry isolation raises his spirits, and he is soon ready to confront his father a second time. On the first occasion in the potato field, his single blow to old Mahon's head was struck in desperation, after his father had provoked him beyond endurance. His heroic account of that confrontation in Act Two, where he imagines himself and old Mahon as two warriors in an epic conflict, is wildly exaggerated. Mahon provides a more plausible account, which features Christy as a cowardly aggressor delivering a sudden blow and running away ('Weren't you of racing the hills before I got my breath with the start I had seeing you turn on me at all?').

Now that Christy is cornered, he is ready to give a factual display of the heroism which had previously only been the product of his heightened imagination. He runs at his father with the loy ('I'm going, but I'll stretch you first'), knocks him unconscious and leaves him for dead. After this, the father-son relationship can never be the same. Mahon seems to want an alliance of equals with Christy as they prepare to leave the shebeen for ever ('my son and myself will be going our own way, and we'll have great times from this out telling stories of the villainy of Mayo and the fools is here'). Christy, however, will have none of this. Now that he has finally conquered Mahon, he feels that the time has come to reverse their earlier roles and for him to assert a total dominance over his father. From now on, he will be the 'gallant captain' and old Mahon his 'heathen slave'. His father will perform menial tasks for him ('stewing my oatmeal and washing my spuds').

RESONANCES OF THE OEDIPUS THEME

Synge's treatment of the father-son relationship in *The Playboy* inevitably calls to mind the Oedipus theme, which Western literature inherited from ancient Greek drama, and of which there are unmistakable echoes in *Hamlet*. The great dramatic hero Oedipus was condemned by the fates to kill his own father and marry his mother. In *The Playboy*, the hero, despite two attempts, falls short of committing parricide, and can only achieve the status of a mock-Oedipus. The main action of the play can be seen as a mock-heroic parody of the Oedipus theme. Attempted murder becomes an absurd comic device ('Are you coming to be killed a third time, or what ails you now?'). Nevertheless, Christy's badly-managed attempts to kill Mahon have a mythic quality, and stand as symbols of his struggle to liberate himself from his father's dominance.

The other element of the Oedipus story, the marriage of the son to his mother is glanced at in *The Playboy*. Christy's mother is not among

Synge's *dramatis personae*, but the Widow Casey comes fascinatingly close to taking her place. When old Mahon wants Christy to marry this great earthy creature ('two hundredweights and five pounds in the weighing scales'), our hero is appalled. It is significant that his principal objection to a union with the Widow Casey carries overtones of possible incest ('all know she did suckle me for six weeks when I came into the world'). By rejecting this woman as a marriage partner, Christy may thus be avoiding the second of the curses of Oedipus (incest) as well as the first (parricide).

Synge's portrayal of the father-son relationship is a subtle one. It is too simple an interpretation to suggest that the dominance of each over the other in turn exhausts the significance of their relationship. There are indications that Mahon, despite the appearance of downright hostility, entertains a suppressed regard for his wayward son. This becomes most apparent as he watches the race with the Widow Quin, Jimmy and Philly. As the race involving Christy is taking place, old Mahon does not recognise his son. Nevertheless, he cannot restrain himself from shouting encouragement as Christy triumphs ('Good rider! He's through it again! ... Good boy to him! Flames, but he's in!'). This may be taken as an instinctive, subconscious expression of parental pride, soon to be dissolved in rage and astonishment as Mahon recognises one of Christy's distinctive mannerisms: 'It's Christy! by the stars of God! I'd know his way of spitting and he astride the moon'.

Language and Imagery

ALMOST every discussion of the language of *The Playboy* has its starting-point in some remarks Synge made in his Preface to the play. Here he declared that in *The Playboy* he had used only one or two words that he had not heard among the country people of Ireland; he had also used a certain number of phrases he heard from fishermen in Kerry and Mayo, or from beggarwomen and ballad-singers. 'Nearly always', he wrote in his programme notes for the first production of the play in 1907, 'when some friendly or angry critic tells me that such and such a phrase could not have been spoken by a peasant, he singles out some expression that I have heard, word for word, from some old woman or child.'

A good example of what Synge is talking about here is to be found in a comparison between a fragment of peasant speech recorded in his book on the Aran Islands and a modified version of the same speech in *The Playboy*. An old islander, Mourteen, told Synge that 'A man who is not married is no better than an old jackass. He goes into his sister's house, and into his brother's house; he eats a bit in this place and a bit in another place, but he has no home for himself; like an old jackass straying on the rocks.' This reappears in *The Playboy* as Michael James pronounces his blessing on Christy and Pegeen: 'What's a single man, I ask you, eating a bit in one house and drinking a sup in another, and he with no place of his own, like an old braying jackass strayed upon the rocks?'

SYNGE'S DEBT TO THE IRISH LANGUAGE

Much of the diction, syntax and idiom in *The Playboy* betrays the unmistakable influence of the Irish language, which has always had a profound effect on the English spoken by Irish people, particularly those of most interest to Synge: peasants, fishermen, tramps and beggars. Synge had a working knowledge of Irish, and many of the proverbial expressions and other sayings in *The Playboy* are direct translations from the Irish:

> I'm thinking
> *Táim ag ceapadh*
> The way I'd have a lovely soft skin on me
> *Sa chaoi go mbéadh craiceann bog mín orm*
> Don't be letting on
> *Ná bí ag ligint ort*
> It'd make the green stones cry itself
> *Bhainfeadh se deora as na clocha glasa*

Sometimes, Synge's debt to Irish is less direct. Some of his best-known lyrical passages are based on Douglas Hyde's translations of *Love Songs of Connacht* and *Religious Songs of Connacht*. Christy's vision of Pegeen ('Amn't I after seeing the love-light of the star of knowledge shining from her brow') owes its inspiration to Hyde's translation of one of Raferty's poems: 'If you were to see the star of knowledge/And she coming in the mouth of the road'. Another of Christy's rapturous exclamations ('Isn't there the light of seven heavens in your heart alone, the way you'll be an angel's lamp to me'), has a similar source: 'And I thought after that you were a lamp from God/Or that you were the star of knowledge going before me and after me' *(Ringleted Youth)*. The most memorable example of Synge's indebtedness to Hyde's translations is his use of two lines from the English version of *Una Bhán:* 'I had rather be beside her on a couch, ever kissing her/Than be sitting in heaven on the chair of the Trinity'. Synge makes Christy talk to Pegeen of 'squeezing kisses on your puckered lips, till I'd feel a kind of pity for the Lord God is all ages sitting lonesome in his golden chair'.

RHYTHMICAL PROSE OF *THE PLAYBOY*

Synge's indebtedness to Irish speech and literature is an important scholarly topic, but the significant critical question concerns the effectiveness, or otherwise, of his distinctive use of language as a dramatic medium. There has been much critical debate about the realism of the language of *The Playboy*. Synge himself, while he claimed that the diction of the play and many of its phrases faithfully reflected the actual speech of country people, did not suggest that his *language* was realistic. It may well be true that the play does not contain any word or phrase not actually used by peasants and fishermen, but, as L. A. G. Strong has pointed out, 'the language of Synge's plays is not the language of peasants, insomuch that no peasant talks consistently as Synge's peasants talk'. A moment's reflection on almost any of the speeches will confirm the truth of this observation. Consider Shawn Keogh's refusal to confront Christy:

> I'll not fight him, Michael James. I'd liefer live a bachelor, simmering in passions to the end of time, than face a lepping savage the like of him has descended from the Lord knows where. Strike him yourself, Michael James, or you'll lose my drift of heifers and my blue bull from Sneem.

There is little difficulty in imagining a countryman using any of the words used by Shawn in this speech, but it would take a very sophisticated countryman, thoroughly accomplished in literary techniques, to pattern his language as Shawn does here. Real-life peasants, or even real-life aristocrats, do not speak rhythmical prose like this. Shawn's speech is a literary product, heightened and refined to achieve the effect of poetry. It incorporates poetic devices such as alliteration ('I'd liefer live a bachelor ... blue bull'), and metaphor ('simmering in passions'), and has the rhythm and movement of verse. The speeches of all of Synge's characters involve a dazzling manipulation of vowels and consonants such as no group of living people could conceivably sustain for any length of time. It has been remarked that the language of the love-scenes between Christy and Pegeen is poetry untrammelled by the mechanism of verse, although it must be pointed out that many of the most celebrated speeches of the play contain concealed lines of verse, and that Synge makes continuous use of simile, alliteration and assonance:

> That God in glory may be thanked for that!...
> I'll bet my dowry that he'll lick the world ...
> there's wonders hidden in the heart of man ...
> as naked as an ash-tree in the moon of May ...
> a hideous, fearful villain, and the spit of you ...
> I felt them making whistles of my ribs within ...
> I've lost the only playboy of the Western World ...

THE RICH IMAGERY OF THE PLAYBOY

The imaginative quality of *The Playboy* is enriched by vivid poetic imagery. In keeping with the varying moods of the play, some of this imagery is grotesque, some of it exotic, and all of it impressive. Synge's images invariably convey a quick sense of the excitement of life on the part of his characters; everything that happens or that may happen appears of vital importance, worthy of being described with the utmost enthusiasm in vigorous, heightened language. To Jimmy's mind, a man who killed his father 'would face a foxy divil with a pitchpike on the flags of hell'. To Pegeen's lively imagination, Christy's 'quality name' would suit the 'great powers and potentates of France and Spain', an exotic idea which stimulates Christy's lively image of his family having proprietorial rights over 'wide and windy acres of rich Munster land'. Sometimes, imagination creates grotesque comic fantasy, as when Christy pictures his father 'rising up in the red dawn' and going out into the yard 'as naked as an ash tree in the moon of May', and 'shying clods against the visage of the stars'.

When the occasion demands, imagery can be deployed for reductive purposes; Pegeen pictures Widow Quin's leaking thatch 'growing more pasture for her buck goat than her square of fields'. Soon afterwards, we have the outlandish image of the Lord Bishop of Connaught feeling the 'elements of a Christian' in a kidney stew featuring a black ram suckled by the Widow Quin. Such flights of fancy appeal to a village audience who compensate for the absence of exciting incident in their daily lives by having recourse to imaginative delights. Hence their willingness to accept and even develop Christy's story of his mighty deed, with all its wealth of pictorial detail.

IMAGES OF CRUELTY AND VIOLENCE

Christy enriches the villagers' understanding of his motives, with a wealth of imagery. He paints a memorable portrait of the grotesque Widow Casey, the woman chosen for him by his father, 'two hundredweights and five pounds in the weighing-scales, with a limping leg on her and a blinded eye'. He evokes the sinister menace of old Mahon who follows him 'like an old weazel tracing a rat', while old Mahon himself uses startlingly violent imagery to convey his demented state: 'There was one time I seen ten scarlet divils letting on they'd cork my spirit in a gallon can; and one time I seen rats as big as badgers sucking the life blood from the butt of my lug'. The cruel plight of those whose minds are disturbed is further enlarged on by Christy with his image of 'the madmen of Keel, eating muck and green weeds on the faces of the cliffs'.

The themes of violence and cruelty, central to the play, are conveyed in unforgettable images. Christy gives various accounts of the slaying of his father, culminating in the highly imaginative picture of old Mahon split open 'to the breeches belt' with a single blow. Jimmy Farrell's cruel hanging of his dog at the end of a string is echoed in Christy's threat to leave Shawn 'hanging as a scarecrow for the fowls of hell'. Some of the images are even more disturbing. The Widow Quin recalls the capture of a maniac by some villagers, who 'pelted the poor creature till he ran out, raving and foaming, and was drowned in the sea'. Mahon remembers the cruelty of old and young towards Christy, and 'they swearing, raging, kicking at him like a mangy cur'.

TENDER IMAGERY

The imagery of the play is not, however, all violent and cruel. There are images of natural beauty and tenderness, particularly in the love-scenes. Christy evokes an ideal world for Pegeen as he imagines the two of them pacing Neifin 'in the dews of night', looking at the little shiny new moon, maybe, sinking on the hills'. He has visions of a wistful God 'sitting lonesome in his golden chair', envying human happiness. He paints a picture of the joyous activity in store for Pegeen and him 'gaming in a gap of sunshine', and conjures up an astonishing image of the holy prophets straining at the bars of Paradise to get a glimpse of Helen of Troy 'and she abroad, pacing back and forward, with a nosegay in her golden shawl'. Another of Christy's images of heaven is more orthodox, and just as beautiful. If the Widow Quin helps him to win Pegeen, he will pray that God will lead her through 'the Meadows of Ease, and up the floor of Heaven to the Footstool of the Virgin's Son'.

THE COMIC EFFECT OF CONTRASTING IMAGERY

Contrast is the basic principle of the style of *The Playboy*. Vivid images of beauty are counterbalanced by equally graphic ones conveying a sense of grotesque ugliness. Christy's delighted, lyrical vision of Pegeen as a saintly, radiant figure, 'with the love light of the star of knowledge shining from her brow', is soon counterbalanced by the gross realism of the Widow Quin's maliciously observed account of Pegeen itching and scratching and reeking of poteen. Sometimes the juxtapositions of incongruous elements can be outrageously comical, as when Pegeen describes Christy as 'a lad with the sense of Solomon to have for a pot-boy'. Violent contrasts like this are used throughout for comic purposes, and produce many a delightful anti-climax. The lyrical tones of Christy's reference to Pegeen as an angel's lamp are quickly dissolved as the same lamp becomes an aid to 'spearing salmons' in the darkness. The blessing of Michael James on Christy and Pegeen juxtaposes references to God, Mary and St Patrick with speculation on grandsons as 'gallant little swearers' or 'puny weeds', a comparison between a single man and 'a braying jackass', and an invocation of divine help for a man who 'split his father's middle with a single clout'.

Synge exploits the comic effect of incongruous juxtaposition most memorably in Pegeen's remark that Shawn would make a girl think about a bullock's liver rather than about a lily or a rose, and in Shawn's indifferent account of his attractions as a suitor: 'And have you no mind of my weight of passion, and the holy dispensation, and the drift of heifers I am giving, and the golden ring?'. Synge's continuous willingness to counterbalance dignified and serious elements with ludicrous and trivial ones gives the comedy its distinctive mock-heroic quality, and makes it difficult to sustain the more solemn interpretations of its significance.

Examining the Play

A) FOR DETAILED DISCUSSION

ACT 1
(Lines 1-113)
1. This passage conveys some idea of Pegeen's attitude to Shawn. How would you describe this attitude?
2. Pegeen and Shawn are sharply contrasted. In what ways?
3. Why is Pegeen prepared to marry Shawn?
4. How would you describe Shawn on the evidence of this passage?
5. Consider the significance of Pegeen's contrast between the men of the past and those of the present.

(Lines 114-219)
1. Discuss the relationship between Pegeen and Michael James.
2. Michael James has one main concern. What is this?
3. What is the significance of the various references to Father Reilly and the other religious figures?
4. Examine the comic aspects of this scene.
5. What is the point of the Pagan-Christian references?

(Lines 220-445)
1. There is comic irony in Christy's first greeting. Explain.
2. Christy refers to himself as the son of a strong (wealthy) farmer. Why do you think he does this?
3. Christy's answers to the various questions about his deed have a comic aspect. Elaborate.
4. Synge's presentation makes it difficult to take Christy's deed seriously. Why is this?
5. Christy is gradually surprised by the reception the villagers give him and his story. Why do they respond so favourably to him?
6. Show how Christy grows in confidence as the scene develops.
7. Examine the role played by Pegeen in this scene.
8. What is Pegeen's attitude to Christy? How does it develop as he tells his story?
9. The scene is full of comic paradoxes. Discuss some of the main ones.

10 Christy later pays tribute to 'the power of a lie' in launching him on his career as a hero. How does lying help him in this scene?

(Lines 446-584)
1 This scene has a vital influence on the growth of Christy's self-esteem. Show how Pegeen contributes to this.
2 Consider the main features of the developing relationship between Christy and Pegeen.
3 What kind of image of Christy is Pegeen in the process of creating? What is Christy's response to this image?
4 How reliable is Christy's account of his father?
5 This scene ends with a comic anti-climax, the first of many. How does this one compare with the others?

(Lines 585-725)
1 What kind of impression does the Widow Quin make?
2 What evidence is there that Pegeen regards the Widow Quin as a threat?
3 In what important way does the widow's view of Christy differ from Pegeen's?
4 What is the significance of Pegeen's satirical comments on the widow?
5 What does the encounter with the widow mean to Christy?

ACT 2
(Lines 1-215)
1 Christy has changed significantly since his first appearance in Act 1. In what ways?
2 What influence do the village girls and the widow exert on Christy?
3 Discuss the impact of Christy's story on himself and on his listeners.
4 Contrast Christy's new version of his deed with his earlier account. Can you explain the differences between the two?
5 What impression of the village girls do we get from this scene? Examine their attitudes and values.

(Lines 216-377)
1 Describe Pegeen's mood as she interrupts the drinking scene.
2 How has Pegeen's attitude to Christy changed since their last encounter, and why?
3 Why does Pegeen introduce her references to the hanging of a man?
4 The key-word in this scene is 'loneliness'. Examine its use and significance.
5 The mood of the scene changes after Christy's speech beginning 'It's well you know what call I have' (line 308). Comment on the nature of this change.
6 How would you describe the relationship between Pegeen and Christy at the end of this scene?

(Lines 378-503)
1. This scene illustrates some aspects of Shawn's character. Mention the principal ones.
2. What further development of Christy's personality is obvious in this scene?
3. Examine the role of the Widow Quin throughout the play. What are her motives here?
4. Shawn says 'I'm a poor scholar with middling faculties to coin a lie'. Consider the significance of this statement. How is it related to one of the main themes of the play?
5. How does Christy's new version of his deed differ from the previous ones?
6. Consider the comic implications of old Mahon's appearance, paying particular attention to its timing.
7. There is irony in Shawn's presentation of his good clothes to Christy. Explain.
8. Widow Quin's proposals to Shawn reveal something important about her character. What is this?

(Lines 504-597)
1. Discuss Widow Quin's management of old Mahon in this scene.
2. Contrast old Mahon's account of Christy with the new image of Christy that has been created since his arrival at the shebeen at the beginning of Act 1.
3. This scene suggests that there are some resemblances between old Mahon and Christy. Comment on these.
4. Mention some examples of irony in this scene.
5. Discuss the significance of this scene for Christy.

(Lines 598-716)
1. A new relationship now exists between Christy and Widow Quin. Explain.
2. Describe Christy's feelings in this scene.
3. What new aspects of Widow Quin's character are revealed here?
4. Is Widow Quin's interest in Christy as deep as Pegeen's? Explain your answer.
5. Explain Widow Quin's comment at the end of the scene.

ACT 3

(Lines 1-268)
1. The dialogue between Jimmy and Philly, and their later behaviour, reveal contrasts between the two men. Mention these contrasts.
2. Why does old Mahon intervene as he does when Philly is talking about the great skeleton he saw as a young man?
3. Do Jimmy and Philly know that Mahon is Christy's father? Explain.
4. What are Widow Quin's motives in this scene?
5. Explain the widow's strategy for dealing with the threat posed by old Mahon.

6 Comment on the similarities between Mahon and Christy suggested by Mahon's language and behaviour in this scene.
7 Widow Quin calls Christy 'the champion playboy of the Western World'. What does 'playboy' mean here? Look up the other uses of the word elsewhere in the play, and consider any changes of meaning it undergoes.
8 What part does Philly play in this scene?
9 Old Mahon takes a strong interest in Christy's performance in the race. What is the significance of this?
10 Discuss Synge's treatment of old Mahon's 'madness'.

(Lines 269-382)
1 Mention any changes worth noting in Pegeen's attitude to Christy since their last encounter.
2 Are the exchanges between Pegeen and Christy to be treated with complete seriousness?
3 Are there any significant differences between Pegeen at this point and Pegeen as she was at the beginning of the play?
4 Mention some of the comic aspects of this scene.
5 What is the significance of Pegeen's reference to the 'Jew-man'?

(Lines 383-522)
1 How would you describe the contribution of Michael James to this scene?
2 What aspects of the character of Michael James are illustrated in his speech of blessing at the end?
3 Discuss Pegeen's sense of values as implied in her attitude to Shawn and Christy.
4 Consider the significance of Pegeen's reference to the bullock's liver and the lily and the rose.
5 Mention some of the farcical elements in this scene.
6 Explain the irony of Christy's remark that he is 'mounted on the springtide of the stars of luck'.
7 Examine Synge's use of contrast in this scene.

(Lines 523-799)
1 Pegeen's phrase, 'and you nothing at all', is an ironic reminder of an earlier, similar comment of hers. Explain.
2 Describe Pegeen's reactions to her discovery that old Mahon is alive, particularly as these affect her attitude to Christy.
3 Trace the development of Christy's responses to the new situation facing him following his father's re-appearance.
4 What does this scene suggest about the psychology of the crowd?
5 How does the Widow Quin misjudge Christy?
6 Some of Shawn's less desirable qualities are exposed in this scene. Comment.
7 (a) Explain the meaning of Pegeen's reply to Christy's question: 'And what is

it you'll say to me, and I after doing it this time in the face of all?'.
(b) Discuss the irony involved in Christy's second attempt to kill his father.
8   How does Pegeen's cruelty influence Christy's attitudes and conduct, particularly after she begins to blow the fire?
9   Discuss the change in Christy's attitude to his father.
10 In this scene, Christy learns some important lessons. What are these?
11 How does Christy's attitude to hanging change?
12 Is Christy better off or worse off, than he was at the beginning?
13 Discuss Christy's strong tendency to dramatise himself here and elsewhere in the play.
14 What has Pegeen lost or gained at the end?
15 With old Mahon's return on all fours, Synge repeats a favourite comic device. Explain.
16 Discuss Pegeen's feelings about Christy as the play draws to a close. How does he feel about her?
17 Farce abounds in this closing scene. Give examples.
18 How does old Mahon feel about Christy as they both prepare to leave?
19 Explain Christy's last words to the villagers.
20 Do you think Pegeen will marry Shawn Keogh? Explain your answer.
21 What does Pegeen mean by her reference to Christy as 'the only playboy'.

B)   FOR GENERAL DISCUSSION

1   It is largely through language, through his successive accounts of the murder and his self-surprising eloquence in wooing Pegeen, that Christy projects and brings into being one of his potential selves that had until now lain dormant.
2   In *The Playboy,* Christy is truly remade by the power of a lie.
3   At the end of each of Synge's comedies, although the solid citizens are left in command of the stage, our hearts go with such outcasts as Christy and old Mahon.
4   Most comic writing, the world over, sides with normal people and established society against the neurotic, the criminal and the social outcast.
5   The exceptional love of Christy and Pegeen could never prosper in the kind of society for which Flaherty's shebeen is the focal point, and whose typical representatives are Shawn Keogh and Michael James.
6   Violence of word and deed is the most obvious reality in *The Playboy.*
7   One of the major themes of the play is a mind's exploration and discovery of itself.

8   Synge's characters, and the setting in which they are placed, have little or no connection with reality.
9   It is difficult to take anything that happens in *The Playboy* with full seriousness; it is extravagant, absurd fantasy.
10 Synge has written an offensive play; its humour is of such a low and vulgar type as to disgust, not to amuse, any mind of ordinary refinement and good taste.
11 Christy's illusion of greatness is nourished and raised to the heights by a community where the mythology of force is dominant.
12 Christy realises that it is not the deed which has made him glorious in the eyes of the villagers, but the telling of the deed, his exceptional powers as a storyteller and his poet's talk.
13 How are we to understand the playboy — as a little schemer making up a story that he destroyed his father (as the Widow Quin concludes); or a poet and a hero (with Pegeen); or an ugly young blackguard and a stuttering lout (with his father); or an ugly liar who was playing the hero (with Pegeen again) or, (as he found himself) 'a kind of wonder was jilted by the heavens when a day was by'?
14 Loneliness and alienation are major themes of the play.
15 No play has ever been at once so completely tragic and so completely comic as *The Playboy*.
16 The play traces Christy's development from dependence on his father, through dependence on his first love, to a healthy and mature self-sufficiency.
17 Love is not the main theme of *The Playboy;* Synge is much more concerned with the opposition between youth and age, and with the conflict between the individual and the group.
18 Synge is more interested in making his audience laugh than in expressing deep or serious thoughts.
19 Ugliness, violence, cruelty and suffering add a grotesque dimension to the comedy of *The Playboy*.
20 The religious motif of *The Playboy* is of major significance.
21 Synge uses dramatic contrast throughout the play, with great skill and resourcefulness. Almost every speech creates a new situation, or farcically reverses its predecessor.
22 With the exception of Shawn, and, presumably, Father Reilly, everyone living in the small, remote Mayo village is stifled by the drabness of existence and longs for action and excitement; it is this that gives Christy his big opportunity to become the village hero.

Critical Comment

1 If what I hear is true, that the audience accepted your play gleefully up to the last five minutes of the third act, I confess to sympathising with the audience. Your play does not end, to my thinking, satisfactorily. Your end is not comedy, it ends on a disagreeable note, and that is always a danger, especially when one chooses parricide as the subject of a jest.

George Moore

2 There was a battle of a week. Every night protestors with their trumpets came and raised a din. Every night the police carried some of them off to the police courts. Every afternoon the paper gave reports of the trial before a magistrate who had not heard or read the play and who insisted on being given details of its incidents by the accused and by the police ... There was a very large audience on the first night ... Synge was there, but Mr Yeats was giving a lecture in Scotland. The first act got its applause, and the second, though one felt that the audience were a little puzzled, a little shocked at the wild language. Near the end of the third act there was some hissing. We had sent a telegram to Mr Yeats after the end of the first act 'Play great success'; but at the end we sent another — 'Audience broke up in disorder at the word shift'.

Lady Gregory

3 As presented at first, I regarded it as a seriously meant contribution to the drama. It now appears as an extravaganza, and is played as such. And yet it lacks the essentials of an extravaganza. The continuous ferocity of the language; the consistent shamelessness of all the characters (without exception), and the persistent allusions to sacred things made the play even more inexcusable as an extravaganza than as a serious play. I prefer to regard it in the latter sense, in justice to Mr Synge's undoubted power as a writer. As a serious play it offends many people; as an extravanganza, it is made peculiarly vile by the many serious allusions to things which Catholic and Protestant hold sacred.

D. J. O'Donoghue

4 It is Pegeen's tragedy ... Christy, like a poet, thinks it is his; and after he has done his best to quench his father with a second blow of a loy, he thinks, poor fool, she will be giving him praises, the same as in the hours gone by. But Pegeen has learnt her lesson; the playboy whom she has been lacing in her heartstrings is only talk indeed. Old Mahon may come in again to be killed a third time, and, seeing Christy bound, and the others busy burning his leg with a sod of turf, may stand up for his son; they may go of together to tell stories of the villainy of Mayo, with Christy turned a likely gaffer in the end of all, while the men return to their drinks; but the curtain will fall upon the grief of Pegeen for an only playboy lost.

P. P. Howe

5 Pegeen is another of Synge's passionate, disturbed women hungry for freedom and romance, and she comes closer to success than her predecessors. Nevertheless, her pride and the fundamental puritanism of her temperament make it impossible for her to accept the consequences of her own dream. She cannot accept the Romancer that is Christy, nor can she face his loss without grief. She represents an Ireland that, dreaming of independence, cannot accept the consequences of the dream becoming reality any more than the faith in spiritual power to which she gives lip service.

For Christy is a representative of faith and spiritual power. He will be 'master of all fights from now', because of that faith. Poverty of spirit is the disease Pegeen and all Ireland must recognize.

Robin Skelton

6 It seems that having come so far Christy is to fail at this last extremity; dream and actuality will disintegrate just as they were about to become one. Then (by a masterly piece of dramatic irony) Pegeen, this time against her will, saves Christy, and makes the transformation complete. Previously her admiration and affection had inspired Christy; now her coldness, her unjust taunts, move him to resolute and effective action. She calls him a 'saucy liar', and co-operates with Shawn to torture and capture him. At this Christy's spirit bends to his full height, and he becomes completely transformed.

Alan Price

7 *The Playboy of the Western World* presents essentially the vision of a man constructing himself before our eyes. Not only does Christy construct himself: he creates his princess. Pegeen is, after all, a matter-of-fact girl with a hot temper. But she is not that sort of girl after a conversation with Christy. As Christy's images grow more and more compelling, Pegeen becomes more and more gentle and eloquent herself. She, too, seems to be changing before our eyes. Finally she comments on the phenomenon: 'And to think it's me is talking sweetly, Christy Mahon, and I the fright of seven townlands for my biting tongue. Well, the heart's a wonder.' But it seems to be the sheer power of language that has won Pegeen, and she apparently recognizes the fact herself when she says she'd not wed Shawn, 'and he a middling kind of scarecrow, with no savagery or fine words at all.'

Patricia Myer Spacks

8 The farcical substratum of the early drafts remained in the completed text, where Christy is led on by easy stages to claim that 'he cleft his father with one blow to the breeches belt'. We watch with delight as the blow, through successive versions of the story, travels down the old man's anatomy. Each new outrage against our sense of truth adds to our feeling that the author is testing the limits of Christy's powers of fantasy and the stage audience's capacity for credulity. As in *Henry IV Part 1* where Falstaff creates eleven adversaries out of two in the space of five minutes, we wait expectantly for the balloon to burst. Christy, in fact, is deflated again and again.

Nicholas Grene

9 His evolution from what his father brutally but succinctly describes as a dribbling idiot, not merely into 'a likely man' but into a poet-hero, 'the only playboy of the Western World', is rapid but sure. So sure that when the reversal comes the new Christy is capable of ousting the original and perpetuating itself. It is the favouring atmosphere of a world of fantasy-builders that starts the process, a world in which whatever is unknown is presumed to be magical and where no talker is without honour provided he has the luck or sense not to carry on his craft in his own country. Christy creeps into Flaherty's inn and the fostering warmth is enough.

Una Ellis-Fermor

10 The early Irish audiences of *The Playboy* objected that the peasants were not pious enough, and therefore untrue. Today, a different form may be given to the objection. The peasants of Synge are not 'true' in any sense; they are literary fictions, like the language imputed to them — a language made up, no doubt, of elements that really occurred, but made up into a state of chemical purity that is quite remote from anybody's real speech.

G.K. Hunter

11 Synge's satiric view is constantly focused, with more or less directness, towards certain aspects of the peculiar blend of paganism and Roman Catholicism that he saw in the West ... Against settled and dull convention and a religion which can be made to appear superficial, there are set Synge's tinkers, tramps, fishermen, publicans, in their actual or potential vitality.

T. R. Henn

12 In an Ireland of plaster saints, Father Reillys and Shawneens, Synge offers the pantomime imp, Mahon's looney. The bathetic device employed in Christy's entry is the foundation of the entire action of the play which, with classic economy, is built merely on varying this incident. Every time Christy rises higher it is to fall lower.

Malcolm Kelsall

13 One of the most inflexible and unhelpful critical attitudes involves the detection of concealed analogies. Christy Mahon, it has been claimed, is a parody version of Cuchullain — or at least has done a deed equivalent to Cuchullain's in modern peasant terms. Or Christy the parricide is a mock Oedipus, and the structure of *The Playboy* is matched point by point with *Oedipus Rex*. Even more often, the playboy has been seen as a Christ figure. Beginning with the argument that Christy's progress is an analogue for Christ's, a scapegoat who can, however, only save himself and not the world, the theory is elaborated to the point where one critic claims that it is through his exploitation in *The Playboy* of the ministry and crucifixion of Jesus that Synge crystallised the elements of his play into a coherent masterpiece. What is wrong with this sort of criticism is that it is quite unrelated to the actual experience of *The Playboy*.

Nicholas Grene

14 Among the impulses behind Christy's mainly instinctive desire to make himself like the image that has been presented to him, the conscious drive has been the wish to impress Pegeen. She played a major part in exciting his imagination with this image, and he wishes to prove to her (as well as to himself) that he really is the same as the image. In this shaping process he is getting into touch with actuality, and becoming aware of certain powers in his nature which were lying dormant until the force of the imagination brought them into activity. Now, faced by Pegeen's anger, Christy experiences a kind of fear and distress unknown to him before; if she withdraws her protection and inspiration he feels that he will never make the image actual, and that he will undergo pain and disappointment unexperienced previously. His character is developing rapidly, and accordingly the opportunities for happiness and sorrow, the rewards and punishments are becoming greater. He is in the middle way; he can never go back to his former undeveloped condition, and his new personality is only in the process of being formed. He still needs the right audience and the stimulus of Pegeen's admiration.

Alan Price

15 It is with Pegeen Mike, the Widow Quin and Christy Mahon that we should be most concerned. Pegeen Mike differs from the other girls in the energy of her passions, the liveliness of her tongue, and the decisiveness of her temper. Rejecting Shawn Keogh, she also rejects the paternal authoritarianism of the Church, as she, too, pays little heed to the authority of her own father. Attracted by Christy, she uses him to further her search for identity, freedom, and romance, finding his words and his deeds heroic and poetic. When old Mahon returns to life she is angered by having been fooled. When old Mahon is killed the second time and Christy set upon and tied, it is she who leads in the tying and it is she who ruthlessly burns him with the lighted turf. Pegeen's intensity of feeling leads her towards both total acceptance and total rejection. Her spirit is akin to the playboy's in its extreme vitality, and it is this that attracts her to him and also causes her to reject him.

Robin Skelton

16 Yet Christy realises that it is not the deed which made him glorious, but the telling of the deed, the 'poet's talking'. And this he retains. He goes out from the community confident in his new strength, but he acknowledges that it is the community which made him ('you've turned me a likely gaffer in the end of all'). It is not only Christy who is transformed: the community itself has made something. Their hero may go from them, but he is their creation — 'the only playboy of the Western World'. A new world is projected into a new orbit.

Raymond Williams

17 Christy eventually lets out that he has killed his father by striking him down with a heavy spade. Instead of this confession being received with horror, Christy finds himself the object of awed admiration, especially by Pegeen. The word 'father' after all, expressed the essence of authority to the peasants, and to kill one's tyrannical father (symbolically) was to achieve the emancipation from authority which every peasant craved. At the same time, with its fear of authority and of desperate men alike, the community chiefly respects those who have the native force to take care of themselves and of those attached to them.

Christopher Gillie

18 Christy has undergone one transformation, from the timid, frightened boy who struck his father only under desperate provocation, into a village hero; he is not to be reduced again. Instead, he becomes a third kind of man: he fights himself free of the villagers and assumes the bullyhood that is his father's style.

Christopher Gillie

19 The villagers turn Christy into a living legend. Their need for a legend, for a mythological hero to give meaning to their own lives, is treated with the ironic sophistication of a modern, critical mind. Christy and the villagers are victims of each other, but at the end of the play, while the villagers return disillusioned to their ordinary, frustrated lives, Christy really has been transformed. Through the imagined experience of a heroic role, into which he is seduced by the villagers, Christy discovers a new faith and confidence in himself: the true myth which informs his progress through the play is the modern, Freudian version of the Oedipal wish to murder the father. The play celebrates the power of the imagination, not to deceive, but to express a hidden, ultimate reality; and Christy achieves the truth, not by rejecting the illusion but by finding that it has emancipated his formerly inhibited self.

D. J. Palmer

20 *The Playboy* was denounced by Dublin for its theme of parricide, but the fact is that, while it makes its comedy from audacious, close looks at the Oedipean struggle between father and son, it ends with the father and son united. It is a play of the discovery of the unknown father, a figure outwardly stingy and gigantically repressive, but lit at the centre by rough family love. Christy's early speeches show his fear and anger with his father, but also his inner warmth.

Herbert Howarth

21 That such a play should have been conceived and written is strange enough; that it should be accepted, rehearsed and enacted at a house supposed to be dedicated to high dramatic art and truth would be past all belief but that has actually been done. The worst specimen of stage Irishman of the past is a refined, acceptable fellow compared with that imagined by Mr. Synge, and as for his women, it is not possible, even if it were desirable, to class them. Redeeming features may be found in the dregs of humanity. Mr. Synge's *dramatis personae* stand apart in complete and forbidding isolation.

The Freeman's Journal, 28 January, 1907

22 Now this Christy, a curious-looking little scamp, is an object upon whom the Widow Quin and two or three other girls have set their affections. What they could possibly have seen in him would have puzzled the indifferent; and why, above all, they should excite each other's jealousy over a self-confessed parricide, the author alone can explain. It can scarcely be true that Irish girls contend for murderers as husbands.

Daily Express, 28 January, 1907

23 *The Playboy of the Western World* is described as a comedy, but its humour is of such a low and vulgar type as to disgust, not to amuse, any mind of ordinary refinement and good taste. This does not apply, I hasten to say, to the first act, which contains much genuinely humorous writing, and which was received with general applause by Saturday night's audience. But the second and third acts were listened to with growing impatience and irritation. As another spectator put it to me, they are written 'in the language of the gutter, with just a touch of quaintness'. The quaintness could not long keep at bay the disgust of the spectators at the growing coarseness of the dialogue.

Francis Sheehy-Skeffington

24 Murder is not pleasant, but what of the other crime — that of a father forcing his son to marry a woman he hated? Were it not for this crime, the other could not have followed. A real, live man was new and fascinating to Pegeen; even a parricide, and the man who had killed his father, rather than marry the woman he hated, might at least be capable of loving sincerely. Then, he was a man who had achieved something, if only murder, and he had achieved the murder obviously because his better character had not been permitted to govern him. When trembling idiocy tends to be the standard of life, intelligence and courage can easily become critical, and women do not like trembling men. In their hearts, they prefer murderers. What is a woman to do in conditions of existence that leave her a choice between the cowardly fool and the courageous criminal?

Patrick Kenny in *The Irish Times,* 30 January, 1907